Hamlet: Do you see yonder cloud that's almost in shape of a camel?

Polonius: By th' mass, and 'tis: like a camel, indeed.

Hamlet: Methinks it is like a weasel.

Polonius: It is backed like a weasel.

Hamlet: Or like a whale.

Polonius: Very like a whale.

Chasing the Sun:
A Journey in Neolithic Speculation

Frederick G. Jones, Jr.

Chasing the Sun: A Journey in Neolithic Speculation
By Frederick G. Jones, Jr.

Book Design by Siri Jones
Printed by Lulu.com

Published by PlumbBob Publishing
358 Main Road South
Hampden, Maine 04444

First Edition
2009

ISBN 978-0-578-04720-1

Copyright © 2009 by Frederick G. Jones, Jr.

All Rights Reserved. No part of this book may be reprinted or reproduced or utilized in any form or by any electronic, mechanical or other means, now known or hereafter invented, including photocopying and recording, or in any information storage or retrieval system, without prior permission in writing from the Publisher.

CONTENTS

Preface......vi
Glossary......viii
Map of the Isles......x
Map of the Orkney Islands......xi
Introduction......xiii

Chasing the Sun: A Journey in Neolithic Speculation......1
The Cup and Ring as Tool......3
The Macehead as Tool......7
The Theory Augmented......13
Scotland Tour IV 2007......15
The Corrimony Cairn......19
The Clava Cairns......21
The Orkneys......25
The Village of Skara Brae......28
Speculating at the Ring of Brodgar......30
The National Museum of Scotland......35
The Bedstead Carvings at Skara Brae: Lines of Orientation......39
The Tripods Depicted in the Stones?......43
Naturalistic Vistas on the Bedsteads?......44
The Large Orkney Stone......46
Back to the Ring of Brodgar......49
And Down to Stonehenge......52
The Stonehenge Macehead at Station Stone 92......55
Over to Ireland and Newgrange......56
Newgrange: Kerbstone 52......59
Lattices and Spirals and Shamanism......61
Who was in Charge?......64
All Together Now: The Neolithic Power Tool Kit......73
References......77

Preface

It is with more than a little trepidation that this theory is offered in print. The author is not an archeologist, has never made a scatter graph, has never wielded a trowel, except in his own garden here in Maine. We amateurs are constantly warned by all the most esteemed in the field of archeology that any attempt to "walk in the shoes" of a Neolithic is nothing short of "delusional." Especially when the walking is undertaken by someone who is a rank amateur. I will have to plead guilty as charged. Yet in my defense, I would recall that *delusion*, (from Latin *ludere*) does contain the primary denotation of 'to play,' and if our experiments on this *journey* seem more like play, playing at what we could s*peculate* with our own eyes, and if the exercise of following the argument presented here is both useful and pleasurable, especially for the amateur reader, then we shall press on and lay out the course of the journey. We will admit to walking in the shoes, speculating as best we can, with just our eyes, using only the tools available at the time. We understand that the earth's axis has shifted over the past 4,000 years, and that our North Star was not at north four millennia ago, and that, consequently, all the declinations of the risings and settings of the sun and moon must be calculated to determine the actual point on the horizon of an event in, say, 2,000 BC. But we won't go there just yet.

To any archeologist, this little book is not technical in any sense. The more arcane bits are found in square brackets, and may be omitted should the reader get that far. The measurements and angles and triangles that we present are accurate as far as we could determine. And we understand that ultimately all our speculations are based on the work of others. We are most cognizant of and grateful for the brilliant work of excavation and reporting that underlay all of our experiences at the sites and in the museums, remembering especially the work in the trenches and the labs by D. V. Clarke, Alison Sheridan, Stuart Piggott, Colin Renfrew, Richard Bradley, Aubrey Burl, Alexander Thom, Colin Richards, Stan Beckenstall, John Hedges, and Ewan MacKie, to mention only a few of the greats of archeology and astronomy to whom we as students are most indebted, both for the immense physical labour expended by them and for the technical expertise evident in the reports which publish their findings to the world.

I am indebted to Historic Scotland for the use of the photograph of the Skara Brae bedstead stone, and to Kilmartin House, to Tankerness Museum and the Orkney Library, to the Simisons at the Museum of the Tomb of the Eagles, to all the personnel of Historic Scotland, who have been so hospitable and instructive, especially Allan Jones at Maeshowe, to the National Museums Scotland and Dr. D. V. Clarke, Dr. Alison Sheridan, and Helen Osmani for many valuable suggestions, and to the British Museum and the British Library.

Many have encouraged me along the way: my family, friends, and neighbors. Our ever-helpful and most competent John Bapst Memorial High School librarians, Kevin Champney and Cyndee Lutz, who managed to ferret out dozens of obscure articles not available in the State of Maine. Those relatives and friends who read various stages of the publication for proof: My dad at 95, Fred Jones, Sr., Bill Jones, Elsa Cruz, Helene Schmidt, Fritz Schmidt, Scott Burgess (Science Department Head at John Bapst and President of the Bangor Astronomy Society), C. Bernard Robbins, Ann Holland, Carol Chambers, Dr. Esther Rauch, and my granddaughter Ashley Baillie. (I, of course, take full responsibility for the many errors that I am sure have crept silently in here and there.) I am grateful to my granddaughter and fellow traveller Ana Ottoson for her stunning photograph of the Ring of Brodgar on page 72. Many thanks to Megan Stewart, my junior English student, who did excellent original work on the Achnabreck orientations: examining close up the carvings at Achnabreck, designing azimuth grids based on the Stationer's Office diagrams, determining the azimuths of the radial cuts, and making a pie chart of those orientations. And also thanks to Hana Kurniawati, my English III Honors exchange student, who visited us from Indonesia, who speaks five languages, and who drew the beautiful maps and illustrations found in the introductory matter and the text. And thanks to all my students, who made up the four Tours on four trips to Scotland, 2004-2007, and to Ireland in 2008, and who were superb throughout in their curiosity and energy, and were indispensable to the project. Many thanks to all.

I owe special gratitude to our daughters Lisa, who critiqued the book, and to Siri, who designed the book, for their never-failing help and support. And Most Especially to my wife and partner, Judy, who supports all of my hare-brained schemes, but who, thankfully, keeps me grounded. Mostly.

Biographical Note

The author received a Ph.D in Old English from the University of Florida. He has taught in the English Department of SUNY Binghamton, and of John Bapst Memorial High School in Bangor, Maine, for twenty-eight years. He was, until retirement in 2005, Organist-Choirmaster of St. John's Episcopal Church in Bangor for twenty-five years, training a large choir of boys and girls and adults, that toured Britain on four occasions from 1986 to 2001 and sang as Choir in Residence, in seventeen cathedrals and abbeys, including Ely, Lichfield, Durham, Bristol, Edinburgh, and St. Paul's, London. Recordings of the choir have been broadcast on Maine Public Radio and on NPR's "With Heart and Voice."

All of the photographs, except where noted, were taken by the author, using a Nikon D40 SLR digital camera.

Glossary

Alignment: the lining up of three points, a backsight, a foresight, and a point on the horizon where a celestial event occurs (not to be confused with *orientation*)

Azimuth: the number of degrees on the compass, where 0° is N, 90° E, 180° S, and 270° W, and all degrees in between these cardinal points

Backsight: the exact point from which to view a solar or lunar event at the horizon

Cairn: a mound largely built of stones, which may contain a passageway into a central chamber for the purposes of ritual and for the disposal of the bones of the ancestors

Cist: a four-sided box-like structure, sometimes containing the remains of the dead and placed at the center of a stone circle or cairn

Corbelled roof: the projection of each course of stone in a wall so that the courses gradually close near the top, to be surmounted finally by a capstone

Cup and ring: a semi-spherical hole, on average 1 ½ inches in diameter, cut in stone, sometimes surrounded by concentric circles, on average 1 inch apart. A large cup and with several rings could be 12 inches across.

Foresight: the point some distance from the backsight, which is set to make an alignment with the solar or lunar event at the horizon

Goddollies: Venus figurines from the Old Stone Age, 30,000 BC

Granny's skateboard: a piece of plywood approximately 18" by 48" with four sets of wheels like an oversized skateboard, used for sliding in and out of the Isbister Tomb

Haft: a handle; a stick or pole to which a stone tool is attached or mounted

Henge: a circular ditch, sometimes accompanied by a circle of stones as at Stonehenge or the Ring of Brodgar or Avebury

Incising: the repeated drawing of a sharp point over a smooth face or rock for the purpose of making straight lines and designs

Isles, The: after Norman Davies' definition in his history, *The Isles*: Great Britain (England, Scotland, and Wales), Ireland, the Orkneys and Shetlands, and the Isle of Man

Kerbstone: the lowest course of stones at the base of a cairn, sometimes decorated

Lintel: a flat stone set over a doorway

Macehead: a carved and polished, pendent-shaped stone used as a plumb bob in the toolkit of the astronomer-shaman-priest-wise one for making astronomical observations

Major moonrise and set: the northernmost and southernmost rising and setting of the moon that occurs only every 18.6 years

Megalithic: lit. huge stone, referring to the Neolithic and Early Bronze Age practices of using large stones in monumental buildings, e.g. 60 tons each for the large sarsen stones at Stonehenge

Megalithic yard: as calculated by Alexander Thom, 2.72 meters, believed to be a unit of measurement used throughout Neolithic Britain and Ireland

Midden: a compacted trash heap, often dug into and used as part of the wall of a Neolithic house

Neolithic: lit. New Stone Age, c. 4,000 BC to 2,000 BC in Britain; stone age farmers, living a more or less sedentary life based on domesticated plants and animals, and hunting and fishing

Orientation: the point (azimuth) on the compass where a celestial event is observed

Orthostat: a large upright stone, either as a single standing stone or as part of the fabric of a Neolithic building such as Newgrange

Outcrop: a flat, open, fairly level rock face devoid of vegetation

Pecking: the use of a sharp stone point and a hammer to peck out bits of stone in the making of curvilinear or bas-relief designs in rock faces

Radial cut: an incision cut from the cup through the several rings, showing the radius of the concentric circles and pointing to the foresight of a significant astronomical event

Recumbent stone circle: a circle of orthostats with two large stones flanking a large stone placed on its side at some point of orientation with an astronomical event viewed from the center of the circle

Roofbox: a rectangular opening above the entrance of a passage tomb which permits the direct beams of the sun to enter the passage only on certain days of the year: at Newgrange, for example, around December 21 at sunrise

Sarsen stones: from saracen, a general term in the early Middle Ages for Muslims or any pagan, heathen, or Wiccan, such as Merlin, who was believed to have brought the stones (and the magic) from Ireland to build Stonehenge upon Salisbury Plain. Sarsen stones are sedimentary, harder than granite, and were transported in the late third millenium from near Marlborough, twelve miles away, to the present site of the monument.

Scop: an Anglo-Saxon poet, from the word "to shape"

Solstice: lit. sun-stops; the apparent stopping of the sun's journey for the few days around December 21, with the SE rising sun and the SW setting sun of the same day, and around June 21, with the NE rising sun and the NW setting sun

Station Stones: the original stones that formed a rectangle to mark the sightlines for the summer solstice rise and the major southeastern moonrise at Stonehenge. The stones themselves have been removed, but the sockets in the chalk indicate clearly where they stood in 2800 BC

Torc: a flat neckpiece made of gold or bronze in the form of the new moon; bands of wires twisted so as to form a neckpiece that would hook at the back of the neck

Trilithon: one of five sets of the largest stones at Stonehenge, set in a horseshoe, the three stones of which look like the Greek letter pi, with two uprights and a lintel

Uroborous: the self-eating animal; in La Tène art a symbol of "process" or rebirth

The Isles

1. Achnabreck, Argyllshire
2. Kilmartin, Argyllshire
3. Nether Largie South Cairn, Argyllshire
4. Temple Wood, Argyllshire
5. Kilmichael Glassery, Argyllshire
6. Ballochroy Standing Stones, Argyll and Bute
7. Long Meg and Her Daughters, Cumbria
8. Newgrange and Knowth, County Meath
9. Loughcrew, Country Meath
10. Fourknocks, North County Dublin
11. Bryn Celli Dhu, Anglesley, Wales
12. Whispering Knights, Oxfordshire
13. Avebury Henge, Wiltshire
14. Stonehenge, Wiltshire
15. Bush Barrow, Wiltshire
16. Folkton Drums, North Yorkshire
17. Edinburgh
18. Towie Stone, Aberdeenshire
19. Clava Cairns, Invernesshire
20. Corrimony Cairn, Invernesshire
21. Callanish, Isle of Lewis
22. The Orkney Islands

The Orkney Islands

1. Skara Brae Village
2. Barnhouse Village
3. Ring of Brodgar
4. Maeshowe Tomb
5. Unstan Tomb
6. Cuween Hill Tomb
7. Wideford Hill Tomb
8. Kirkwall
9. Hill of Hellias, Hoy
10. Isbister Tomb of the Eagles, South Ronaldsay
11. Eday Manse Stone, Eday
12. Pierowall Stone, Westray

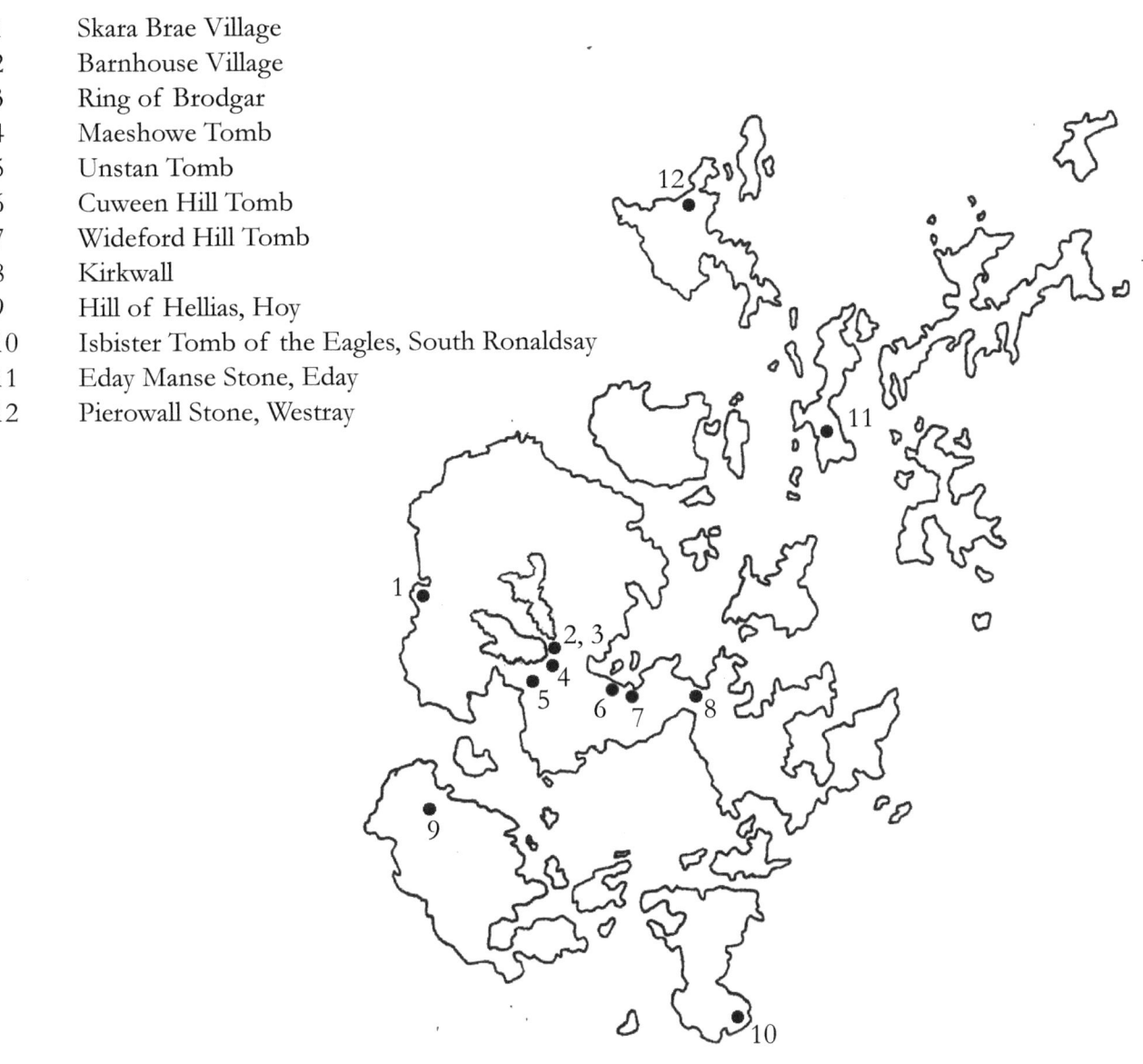

Cup and four rings with radial cut at Achnabreck (photo: Ana Ottoson)

Introduction

So, boys and girls, where does the sun come up in the morning? In the east, you say? Well, yes. But exactly where in the "east"? And how do you know?

These are questions I have asked my students for several years, and virtually none can give a suitable answer. "East" is good enough for us. But in the old days, the Egyptians, the Mayans, the Early People of Britain and Ireland were so obsessed with these questions that they built the Egyptian and Mayan pyramids and hundreds of British and Irish "stonehenges" and tombs, each involving exquisite planning and enormous expenditure of energy, moving tons of gargantuan stones—efforts that tax even our most valiant attempts at replication using modern machinery. And they accomplished these heroic feats just to memorize for themselves and their descendents the answers to these questions. But for what larger purpose? What drove these massive undertakings?

Archeologists are attempting to answer these questions, but the rest of us just stare at the sheer size of the monuments. Stonehenge is ubiquitous in television and print advertising. We all recognize those gigantic sarsen pillars. Tens of thousands of tourists visit the site every year. Decades of work have been devoted by archeologists, work still in progress, to the understanding of its origins, its many stages of building and rebuilding, and ultimately its purpose. Millions of pounds will be spent in the coming years to ensure its preservation and access. And *National Geographic* feeds the popular imagination with Stonehenge articles every few months.

Archeological studies have demonstrated that the orientation of Stonehenge—its ditches, its Heel Stone, its so-called trilithons (see the Glossary)—are set to the summer solstice sunrise and winter solstice sunset. Other parts of the monument are oriented to the much more complex 18.6 year lunar cycle. Indeed, most megalithic monuments are oriented to some or another "important" solar or lunar event. The entranceways into several important monuments—the great Knowth Tomb in Ireland, Cuween Hill Tomb in Orkney, and the Stones of Callanish in the Outer Hebrides—are oriented due east and west, right where the sun makes its first appearance and disappearance on the equinox dates. Now *we* know that the equinox occurs around the 21st of September and the 21st of March with the sun rising due east and setting due west. But the Early People had no clock and no calendar and, therefore, had no way of determining that the night was equal to the day. Did they reckon the months? Have a March or a September? They knew summer and winter's heat and cold. Their senses told them that. But what was the need for orienting to the equinox, of all things, and how did the Early People determine this orientation? How did they even know due east and west? Why did they orient east and west? What was the motivation for building in the first place?

For students of the Early People, these are important questions. As a layman in the field, I have spent more than a few years visiting prehistoric sites, filming and photographing them, as well as studying some of the vast literature on the subject of the Neolithic period. Not only was I fascinated with the tombs and stone circles, but also with the movable artifacts, such as the maceheads and carved balls found in virtually every museum in the Isles, and the carvings found on rock faces and on the megaliths that often make up part of the fabric of these monuments. Many studies organize the artifacts into types, based on common features of design (pestle maceheads, cushion maceheads, Maesmore maceheads, etc.). The same with tombs and circles and stone carvings. But what were the maceheads for? Why were carvings of spirals and lozenges and other abstract designs worked into the standing stones and passageways of the tombs? What about those beautifully polished fist-sized stone balls? Furthermore, what is artistic about so-called "rock art"? Is a cup-like depression carved into a rock face, art? Perhaps we need a workable definition of art for the Neolithic period. Questions remain legion. The information boards that explain these artifacts often use terms like "mystery" or "ritual use." Which means that no one really can say with certainty what they are all about. Would it be too rash to suggest a "forest for the trees" syndrome on the part of the experts? Of course, those comprehensive studies of types do lay the groundwork for the questions of why, when, where, and how. But those questions receive short shrift in the literature on the period. What can't be proved can't be uttered. Speculation is forbidden.

So this book offers a general theory, which came to me out of the blue sometime just before my first student tour in 2004:

- That the cup and ring carvings on open faces of stone are not art, but technology, the purpose of which was to make a permanent point of reference, a benchmark in stone, in the practice of orientation.

- That maceheads were not mounted on sticks or poles as current dogma asserts.

- That maceheads and carved balls were hung as weights from a tripod down to the cup mark and then pulled by the cord to bring the mark on the ground to eye level.

- That the vertical line made by the cord can be made to line up with a second tripod (or a point on the horizon) where a significant solar (or lunar) event could be noted and therefore predicted at a later time, as the sun and moon move back and forth across the horizon.

- That this lining up of two cords (or a cord and a distant point on the horizon) can be adjusted to mark with precision the moment of a rising or setting of the sun or moon and a cup mark cut into the stone below for memory's sake.

Obviously, the first point marked by the cup and its tripod and cord is arbitrary. Step away ten feet and walk in a circle around it and one has traversed the 360 degrees of the horizon. But stop at any point and set up a second tripod, and one has then made an alignment with some point on the horizon, which can then be marked in stone below by another cup. The process is simple enough to have escaped the notice of every archeologist devoted to the subject of alignments. These artifacts, I suggest, are seen here as the tools of the trade of the astronomer and the liturgist and as devices essential to the celebration of the yearly round and the lives of the ancestors. They are not only "symbols of power," as several eminent scholars have asserted, but were physical tools essential to the work of the Early People.

Several ancillary concepts work in concert with this new theory of these artifacts, involving not only the alignments of monuments, but also shamanism and prehistoric geometry, both of which subjects having received considerable attention of late. These concepts are developed as the "journey" progresses through the book.

Chasing the Sun tries to accomplish a number of things at once: It is a telescoped travelogue of trips through the Isles, made with my students, which shows the development of my theory, starting on the southwestern coast of Scotland, up the Great Glen to the Orkney Islands, down to Edinburgh, with side trips to southern England and eastern Ireland. And it is a narrative of experimental archeology, as we tested the feasibility of the theory. Of course, the book ultimately raises more questions than it answers, which will be seen in the last couple of chapters. Yet it is my fervent hope that through this "journey," my students and readers will become more aware of the wonders of the past, of the brilliant and innovative minds of our ancestors, and will understand more clearly our intimate relationship with Mother Earth and the cosmos, a relationship which our forebears celebrated and incorporated into their daily lives.

Now let's head off to Scotland to see what they could see.

Cup and six rings with radial cut in the midst of other cup marks at Achnabreck.

Chasing the sun:
a journey in Neolithic speculation

Macehead model over the "cup with five rings" at Achnabreck near Kilmartin

My Scotland Tour I of some fifteen high school juniors and seniors walked quick-step up from the car park to the Achnabreck cup and ring stone carving site to view the largest stone outcrop covered with carvings to be found anywhere in Britain, an important Neolithic monument, which had been in use for hundreds of years in the third Millennium. The carvings shone in the sharp rain, and our fingers numbed as the tripod was hastily fashioned from three long sticks and a half a megalithic yard of two-inch duct tape. Once the tripod was up, the Ceremonial Macehead was hung from the top of the tripod by a string, dropped to the "cup with five rings" to "backsight" (find an exact point from which to view) the "foresight" (point in the distance)–perhaps a certain crevice in the rock-strewn hills beyond, or the face of a twelve-foot high standing stone some fifty yards away. The radial cut from the center through the rings, pointed to the direction of the foresight and to the point on the horizon. Our macehead was then lifted to eye level.

Sighting through the hole we could see the point at which the last flicker of sunlight on the distant hill would disappear at the sunset. The midwinter sun would have set in the southwest behind the hills beyond the Sound of Jura on the three days or so of the solstice, before it started back on its annual journey north up the horizon to the warmth of summer. However, today was February 24, 2004, more than two full moons after the winter solstice.

If we had been there in late December for the solstice setting in the southwest, the backsight macehead would have been drawn up from the permanent benchmark in the stone, i.e. the cup and ring. And the radial cut would have pointed to a different foresight—at azimuth 215°—a crevice a bit south of the foresight on February 24. For the Neolithic astronomer, the accomplishment of lining up the macehead of the backsight with the point in the distance and aligning that point with the extreme rising or setting of the sun or moon would have been no small feat. And the memory of the event as well as its repetition each year would have led naturally to the need for making a permanent record of the sighting: the first sighting is made, the cup is pounded out at that point, the standing stone is set or the distant crevice is memorized, the radial cut is carved, and each time the sighting is made from that cup, a new ring is added. "A whole history," in the words of Hamlet, may reside hidden in the faces at Achnabreck. And there are thousands of cup and ring carvings throughout the Isles to be studied from this point of view.

This is the gist of the theory: the cup mark is the benchmark, the radial cut points to the general direction of the sighting, the macehead is the backsighting instrument (the Neolithic theodolite), and the tripod enables the macehead to be dropped exactly on the cup mark. When the macehead is drawn up to eye level, the alignment is presented to the eye. The point in the distance beyond, the foresight, marks the second point required in an alignment. Over periods of hundreds of years, the Neolithic astronomers chased the sun back and forth across the horizon, and in that way they got their calendar, as well as, we may reasonably speculate, their pattern of ritual life.

The tripod and macehead at Corrimony Cairn

The Cup and Ring as Tool

Cup and ring carving with radial cut (National Museums Scotland)

    The theory may be understood as having two components, the carving on the rock face and the stone macehead. The first component of the theory is that the single cups, the cup and ring, and the cup and ring with a radius cut, are not primarily "rock art" but rather are benchmarks—akin to the Coast and Geodetic Survey brass bench marks—for the "backsighting" of the alignments and for the application of those alignments to the orientations of the buildings—cairns, henges, stone circles, houses. The cup is the primary benchmark. The radial cut extending from the center of the cup outwards will be read as a pointer to the direction of the foresight crevice of the distant mountain. But the gist of the first component of the theory is that the cup (and its ring) is the backsight tool of the astronomer's trade.

> [The numbers of the rings may be symbolic, representing a hierarchy of wise ones, with the arch-astronomer owning the cup with nine rings; or perhaps revealing the number of occasions on which the cup has been successfully used in astronomical observations; or the mimicking of the concentric walls of certain buildings, which may be oriented to the same event as the cup and ring. Or there may be some sort of calculus amongst the cups and their numbers of rings and even between the orientations of their alignments.]

    Throughout the British Isles and Ireland bald stone outcrops are found, some with scores of carvings of cups from one to three inches in diameter. These cups are very often encircled by concentric rings, from one to as many as seven, and are spaced evenly from the center of the cup. Often a radial cut or two will be found, pecked out or incised from the center of the cup to the outer perimeter.

These designs are also found on mortuary house foundation stones, on orthostats near tombs, as well as on outliers near stone circles, such as Long Meg and her Daughters. However, the largest single collection of such designs in Britain is found at our primary destination on that chilly, blowsy February 14, 2004—at Achnabreck Farm in the southwest Highlands near Kilmartin, in Argyllshire. We took several readings with our tripod and wooden macehead.

The question of the use of these designs, beyond their purported artistic or decorative one, has been raised whenever these artifacts are mentioned in the literature, and many theories have been propounded, some more plausible than others. Stan Beckensall in his study of the prehistoric rock art of Northumbria cites over fifty theories, based on the definitive study by Ronald Morris in *The Prehistoric Rock Art of Galloway and the Isle of Man*. Morris himself lists one hundred-four theories, including bonfire ritual site markers, early pilgrimage marks, star maps, a tattooist's shop and window, basins to catch the blood of the sacrificed lamb, and many more. Over one hundred theories! And in her discussion of "the Neolithic Achievement" Caroline Malone has this to say about rock carvings in her *Neolithic Britain and Ireland*: "Marking the rocks with designs and symbols was a way of identifying them, investing meaning and place in them, and communicating through symbols and signatures of ownership. The rock art consists of zigzags, concentric rings and cup marks, linear and geometric patterns of triangles. *It is never naturalistic in Britain* . . . Instead, the patterns are mysterious, with forms that might be likened to the shapes of henges, houses and passage tomb, to torcs and rings, to the sun, moon and stars and early metal work spirals" (254) [my emphasis]. Malone's phrase "communicating through symbols and signatures of ownership" certainly is compatible with the theory that will be offered here, and her idea that rock art "might be likened to the shapes of henges, etc." also makes a point that we shall elaborate on shortly.

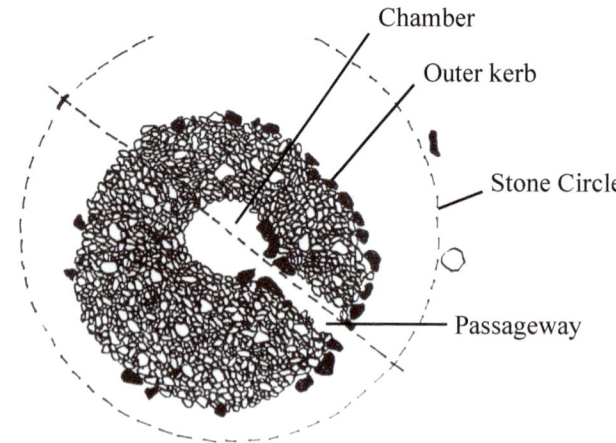

Diagram of passage grave
(Hana Kurniawati after Bradley et al, 2000)

Achnabreck cup and ring mark

Orthostat at Nether Largie South, near Kilmartin   *Cup marks on orthostat near Temple Wood*

Continuing discussion on the proposal that the the cup and rings served as permanent benchmarks for a vertical plumb line raised an issue on a subsequent Scotland tour: why are cupmarks found on the faces of vertical stone outcrops? The answer may be that the nearly vertical "dripping" cupmarks at Kilmichael Glassery, for example, could have been used as benchmarks—if a tripod of two long legs and one shorter leg on the upper horizontal surface suspended a macehead so that it would line up with a cupmark, the foresight cord would be set. With the other tripod set up on the more horizontal surface and the macehead drawn up from the cup and rings marks, the observer would have an alignment.

What if those cups and rings were practice carvings? Perhaps they had over time become iconic, like the cross or the yin and yang or the uroborous in the Book of Kells. The cup marks on the upright stones at Balleymenoch and on hundreds of other standing stones (Long Meg, the Whispering Knights), and the positioning of the cup marks on the upright slab at the cist grave in Nether Largie South, and the orthostats at the Nether Largie or at the junction of the entrance passage and the chamber of the Southwest Clava Cairn, do not militate against the theory.

Moreover, several writers on the subject say that the standing stones, originally prone, were moved and raised after the cup marks were made. Having expended many hours using the cup and rings of, say, a prone Long Meg, and after the stone circle had been made and the various points on the horizon marked with the second tripod, and lined up with the edge of the standing stone (as with the Heelstone at Stonehenge or Ballochroy)—the builders would raise upright the Long Meg, containing the cup or cups and rings and set her up at the major sightline—a memorial, as it were, to the good work of the chief engineer and of the clan as a whole, a symbol of the power of the people. Massive, and virtually immoveable, these stones would inevitably gain in "power" with use, or might have been the perfect memorial with which to honor, for instance, that child buried in the cist at Nether Largie South. That was the substance of the discussion down in the cairn at Nether Largie on April 14, 2007—nine high school students in dank semi-darkness speculating on someone's reason for the particular treatment of a child's body and all the difficult stone work done around and over the cist some 4,000 years ago.

Three views of the Cup and ring marks in the rock outcrops at Achnabrecht near Kilmartin, Scotland

Cup and ring marks in Cairn T at Loughcrew, Ireland

Cup and ring marks (National Museums Scotland)

The Macehead as Tool

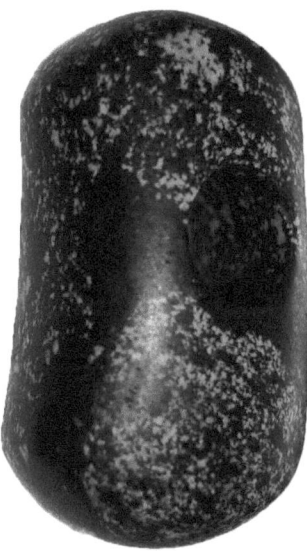

The Isbister Tomb of the Eagles polished macehead. The hole is perfectly round and absolutely smooth to the touch, as is the outside surface. (Tomb of the Eagles Museum, at Isbister on the island of South Ronaldsay)

The second component of the theory is the so-called Ceremonial Macehead, a device which has been seen universally but solely as a symbol of power. It is described by some archeologists as having been mounted on a stick and carried "swaggeringly" by the clan chieftain (Burl, *Avebury* 141). However, I propose that the macehead functioned as a kind of Neolithic theodolite, capable of focusing on a point in the distance and with the cord and tripod, of making a perfectly vertical line based on any benchmark.

[The most recent summary of the dogma that has prevailed for the past half century concerning the macehead and other carved artifacts states that "in the village (of Skara Brae) around the larger houses examples of a strange artifact were found. Small carved stone balls of intricate highly detailed design were used at Barnhouse, and they seem to have been symbolic regalia of some sort. Also found at Skara Brae and in Aberdeenshire, these objects were obviously important, for the more intricate took a long time to make—three days, in modern experiments. The great majority discovered so far come from Aberdeenshire and it is likely that they were first made there. Maceheads . . . have also been found at many sites. . . These are the accessories of religious and political ceremony, like the scepter and orb of medieval and modern kingship, and were probably carried in procession and displayed at important moments" (Moffat 2005, 143).]

So, according to our new theory, the macehead's function was not primarily ceremonial or symbolic, but rather was a tool in the toolbag of the person responsible for determining orientations: the civil engineer (astronomer, shaman, chieftan) of the clan. There must have been many such engineers over the years, as the multiplicity of finds attest.

Concerning the provenance of the macehead, and taking into view the Isles as a whole, we find that the polished macehead is found everywhere, from the Orkneys to the Thames and from East Anglia to western Ireland. Fionna Roe's definitive study of the typology of the macehead (1968) shows that some 275 maceheads have been found in Britain and Ireland, with concentrations in the Orkney Islands and Aberdeenshire. (See also Ritchie's and Simpson and Ransom's more recent discussion in Sharpton and Sheridan.)

In the Orkneys alone, some 74 maceheads have been unearthed, according to A. Foxon in *Neolithic and Bronze Age Finds* [located in the Orkney Library], an unpublished compilation of Orkney's portable artifacts. Curiously, this number of maceheads listed by Foxon matches closely the number of clans, as reckoned by John Hedges some years ago in his *Tomb of the Eagles*. Perhaps the macehead was the collective property of the clan as a whole, one per clan. Or the privileged possession of the leader, and passed down from generation to generation. Of course, some sites have revealed several maceheads each (Barnhouse and Skara Brae), while other sites, only one (Isbister), or none. Yet taking into view the Isles as a whole and Roe's distribution maps of the macehead in Britain, we see that the macehead is found throughout the islands with concentrations at or near large ritual sites. Most writers interpret the macehead strictly as a symbol of power and of no practical use whatsoever. Near the end of her definitive study of the typology of the macehead, Roe says, ". . . mace-heads seem at first, at any rate, to have fulfilled some definite purpose. The uses for which they were made, however, are less easy to infer." And again, "Evidently the manufacture of mace-heads, which was perhaps eventually intended to be ornamental rather than functional, was abandoned in favour of the later varieties of battle-axe."

Three views of a polished macehead

Examples of various shapes of ceremonial maceheads

Amongst the precisely decorated pottery and the polished knives, axes, buttons, and flint handaxes, the polished macehead has no equal. The stone was always exotic and colorful, the shapes were aesthetically perfect, the technical expertise in turning a chunk of raw stone into a polished jewel involved skills of the highest order. And it was eminently useful. Descriptions in the archeological reports hint at the beauty of the macehead. One Barnhouse Orkney macehead is described by Ann Clarke: "Cushion macehead of highly-polished garnet-hornblende gneiss, broken across shafthole, but otherwise in fine condition. Blade end slightly splayed and rounded." And of a macehead discovered north of the Stones of Stennis she noted: "Fragment of highly polished biotite-hornblende gneiss, ovoid macehead, broken across shafthole" (Clarke 331). Also in the same collection of reports from Barnhouse, Richards writes: "Considering the colourful type of stone selected and their highly-polished finish, many maceheads can only be described as very attractive objects. Four maceheads were recovered from within the Barnhouse village, one from Barnhouse Odin and ten from the immediate vicinity of the Stenness and Brodgar henges and a single example from a burial cist in the Stenness parish. Of these, three were complete with the rest being broken, the majority of which were snapped across the shaft hole." As we can see from the many surviving examples, the macehead was the chief jewel of the Neolithic order—having been pains-takingly ground out and rubbed smooth, its maker having drawn out beauty and refinement from raw stone, a rock nearly always variegated and colorful, worthy to be respected, smooth to the touch, and durable in its use. That is, until some new force caused the clans to abandon their traditional ritual practices and to destroy their power tools.

[The Early Bronze Age Bush Barrow Macehead, with its hole cut at the center of the stone, surely could have been carried swaggeringly. But all of the maceheads from our Neolithic period have the hole offset and usually drilled nearer the narrow end, which would allow the macehead to hang straight down, the greater mass being below the hole. (The Bush Barrow Macehead would never have been hung from a cord; the hole is drilled through the center. Furthermore, because the zigzag bone decoration of the haft was found with the macehead, though the wood was gone, it is clear that the Bush Barrow Macehead was mounted.) No hafts have been found with any Neolithic macehead. If the Neolithic maceheads were ever hafted, any evidence of the haft, stick, or pole would have disintegrated long ago, leaving no trace of its existence. The only evidence of hafting will have to be discovered through microscopic study of any abrasions in the macehead hole and sides. Rots' study of hafted tools, unfortunately, does not mention the macehead. Likewise, the tripods would have also disappeared. But unlike the putative haft of the macehead—for which there is no evidence and the mere existence of which we doubt—we do have visual representations of the tripod incised into stone, as we shall soon discover. A comprehensive study of the particular contexts, findspots, based on Fiona Roe's study, of all the extant maceheads, might help in the work to define the processes of transitions that occurred between the Late Neolithic and the Early Bronze Ages. For example, the Isbister mace, discovered by Ronald Simison, buried at the corner of the Tomb of the Eagles. Why there? And why its companions, the polished knives, eagle claws, and jet button. Or the macehead found in the floor of House 2 at Barnhouse. Or the several broken ones found in the vicinity of Barnhouse and the Ring of Brodgar.]

Unfinished and broken maceheads

    The macehead, as tool in the kit of the sun-struck or the "lunatic" astronomer, would have functioned in the same way at every use, a simple but superlative scientific instrument, the use of which reveals understanding of gravity and its use in determining the perfect vertical (the cord), the application of the vertical to the horizontal and from thence to the development of basic geometry and astronomy: the macehead, hung from the tripod—the two instruments working in consort.

> [The uses and strength of the tripod and triangle would have been common knowledge since the time their ancestors had been living in tepees, moving about the countryside in search of game. And they surely understood the uses of the triangle in the laying out of their ritual spaces, as Thom has clearly shown in all his work.]

    Dropped from a tripod, as the macehead is positioned at the cup, after many hours of our engineer's pounding rock to make that mark, and as the macehead is drawn up to eye level, the stone of the macehead, carved from a piece of the earth itself, merges with the landscape and the cup and ring carving on the ground. The sun, the moon, and the stones of earth become one in the eye of the beholder. And if this solar or lunar event be imagined as accompanied with ritual, with intoxicants, with music and dance and drumming, an echo chamber in the tomb, the old people, the young, all doing their part, perhaps then the shamans of the clan, urged by the spiral carvings and the rhythms of the drums, might have begun their journey into the otherworld, dare one say, to meet with the Souls of the Beloved Departed, whose bones had been memorized and so faithfully tended from generation to generation. The combination of drumming, chanting, wailing, and dancing—taken all together, the tribes had a prescription for an enormous celebration.

> [Studies by Chris Scarre and others on the acoustics of enclosed spaces, have revealed the amplifying effect of the kick-back of the stones combined with an ambient resonance of around 60 Hz.]

At this point in our most recent journey through the Isles, we viewed the cup and ring carvings as permanent markers in the ground for making alignment backsights, at a point at eye level precisely above the ground mark. The astronomer sights through the macehead hole to catch the proper foresight, to memorize the point in the distance, in order to mark the significant moment and to make an alignment at a later time with the same significant moment in the sun's journey back and forth across the horizon.

As a corollary to our theory of cup and ring as a tool, we speculated that the full cup and ring with pointer resembles quite clearly the layout of many, if not most, Neolithic buildings: the passage and chamber of the Clava Cairns, of Newgrange, Barnhouse, Maeshowe, Bryn Celli Dhu, as well as the stone circles, Stonehenge, the Ring of Brodgar, Temple Wood. The list could go on and on. The full cup and ring with pointer is a miniature of the predominant ritual and domestic structures of the Neolithic. Researchers (Garnhan, Hodder, O'Sullivan, Bradley [1997], and others) see homologies in the shapes and orientations of the Neolithic house and hearth, tomb, and ceremonial spaces. To that list we would add the cup and ring carving—not only as a miniature work of art, but more importantly as a tool, marking the benchmark and pointing to the foresight. Orienting the world around them.

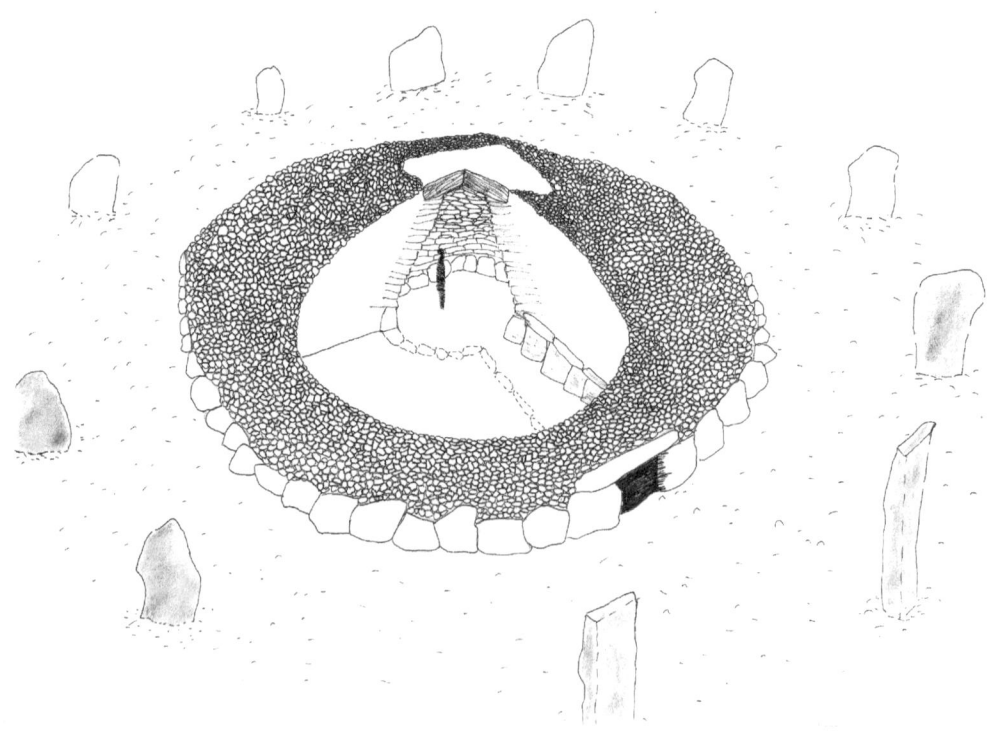

Diagram of Northeast Passage Grave, Clava Cairns (Hana Kurniawati, after Historic Scotland)

The theory augmented

During the course of three years, from 2004 to 2007, we developed some refinements to the theory with the addition of a second tripod, placed a few, as it were, "megalithic" yards away from the first tripod, in the direction of the point on the horizon. The second tripod is now erected between the macehead tripod, which stands over the backsight bench mark (at the eye level of the engineer) and the point on the horizon of the sunset. If a weight, such as a "mystery stone" (one of the fist-sized carved balls, or even another macehead [see Edmonds in *Vessels*]) were to be dropped from the second tripod, and the tripod adjusted so that the string were made to line up with the string of the first macehead tripod, and with a sighting made between the two strings and the distant foresight, then a very accurate alignment, orientation, and record could be made at the site, that would not depend on a distant foresight such as a cleft in the horizon.

Replica of one of the more unusual of the carved balls from Skara Brae (World Heritage Site, Skara Brae)

View of sunrise through two tripods, the macehead, and the "mystery stone"

Two or even three tripods are more accurate than one and thus an alignment could more easily be adjusted to the precise pinpoint of the demise of the light of the sun or moon. This would account for the multitude of cup marks clustered together on certain parts of an outcrop: the astronomers marked in stone their attempts to chase the solstice or major moonrise year after year and therewith kept a record of each year's attempt. Using the same tool-kit down in the valley the next day to orient your mother-in-law's hearth or cairn, or Great Auntie Olga's cist grave, a required orientation could be determined with close to modern accuracy, and the orientation of the houses or tombs themselves could then serve as a solar calendar. Just a quick trip down the hill and across the valley, set up the tripods, and mark the alignments at sunup and sundown. Build the houses on those alignments, and enjoy the full force of the sun filling the dwelling for those few days each year. And similarly with the tombs as well.

> [The studies of Thom, Burl, Ruggles, McKie and others have focused on the question of the precise declination of the solar/lunar rise or set at particular sites, declination being the number of degrees north or south of the celestial equator at which the sun or moon first appears on the horizon, and is determined by the formula *inv sin d = (sin l × sin h) + (cos l × cos h × cos az)*, where *d = declination, l = latitude, h = horizon height, and az = azimuth* (Burl 1997). Our theory is based on what the eye can see. One can observe the northernmost rising of the sun, for example, at its three or four day standstill, regardless if the observer is seeing the sun rise over the North Sea or over a nearby mountain. The sun at solstice will rise earlier on the morning of December 21 over the sea than it rises over a mountain, and it appears to rise further to the south over the mountain on the same day. But without a calendar, or a timepiece, much less the concept of latitude or the celestial equator, the people of the Neolithic period would have thought the preceding sentences meaningless. They would have understood that the solstice viewed from Achnabreck was the same solstice viewed from Temple Wood in the valley of Kilmartin. Even the varieties of horizon and presence of trees should not have prohibited obtaining good sightlines: In the winter distant hills can be seen through the limbs with no leaves, or trees could just have been cut down deliberately as we do now to make a modern scenic highway view. Cummings and Whittle discuss the issue at length. When the sun stops, it stops, wherever the horizon may be. We consider the issue of declination to be irrelevant to our theory.]

Although the distribution maps of chambered tombs (Henshall 2001), recumbent stone circles (Ruggles 1985), stone circles (Bradley 2002), and carved balls (Marshall 1973), show a concentration of each of these in Aberdeenshire and surrounding areas, maceheads, as we have noted, have been found in Neolithic and Early Bronze Age sites throughout Britain and Ireland (Roe 1973). Certainly, through their practical use and the pains that were taken to make them beautiful, they had become symbols of power, but they were more than that. They had become a *power-tool*.

"Mystery Stones" (NMS)

Scotland Tour IV: 2007

So, now we fast forward to April, 2007, with a new group of nine high school students, Tour IV, grades nine through eleven—on a nine-day time-warping trip through the tombs and towns of Western and Northern Scotland.

Back again at the Achnabreck site, with the aid of a hiker's magnetic compass, several readings of the orientation of the radial cuts were made, not geodedically accurate, but suitable for the purpose. Continuing the work while on a smooth sailing to Mull the next day, with the Royal Commission's map of the Upper Face of Achnabreck laid out on the table in the lounge, junior Megan Stewart determined that the majority of orientations fell largely into azimuths spread out between due East and SSW. The lone 25° cut is oriented toward the major northern moonrise; the 35° cut is the summer solstice rise; the 215° cut is the winter solstice set; and the 330° is the major northern moonset. There is a clustering around 125° and 155°, the midwinter sunrise and the major southern moonrise, respectively. The cups with the greatest number of rings match up to the major points on the compass, with the 35° cut at 7 rings, and the 150° and 180° cuts at 6 rings each. The three cuts at 0° contain thirteen rings among them. The three cuts between 150° and 155° contain fifteen rings among them. Perhaps the number of rings is indicative of a system of ranking, as if each carving was "owned" by a particular clan or shaman. Or perhaps the rings indicated frequency of use or accuracy. There is much further study to be done here, since Megan analyzed the cup and rings from the upper face only. A complete inventory of the other Achnabreck faces would be in order, as would a study of the orientations of the hundreds of other decorated stone surfaces throughout the Isles. Unfortunately, most of the illustrations in the several excellent studies on the subject do not as a rule show the north-south orientation.

Megan Stewart figures the approximate azimuth of a large cup and ring carving at Achnabreck, using a simple hiker's compass.

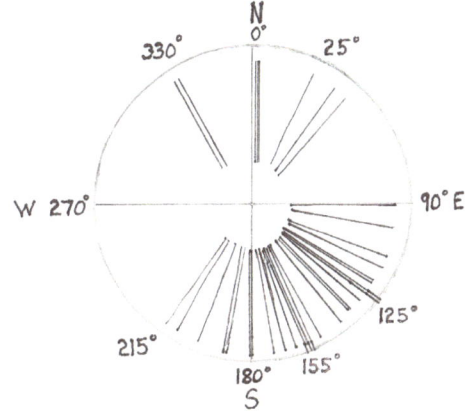

Figure 1. Orientations of the radial cuts of the Upper Face of Achnabreck (Megan Stewart)

Model of the stages of the Temple Wood Cist and Circles. The cairn finally covered all. (Kilmartin House Museum)

Temple Wood Circle and Cist today

A question arose whether there was any correlation between the orientations of the Achnabreck carvings, the monuments at Kilmartin Nether Largie North, and the cist at the center of the circle at Temple Wood. Both tombs have an orientation, according to Aubrey Burl, toward the midwinter setting sun, which fits neatly with the Achnabreck (albeit randomly chosen) azimuth 210° cup and its four rings, and with at least one or two more of those (azimuth 215° with two rings each) of the Upper Face. We noted that the range between 215° and 330° shows no radial cuts, so therefore we speculated that at least two (random!) connections had now been made between the Achnabreck site and the monuments in the valley below, between the cup and ring and the orientation of the cairn. Turning to the north of Scotland, we find that Henshall and Ritchie, in their discussion of the orientations of the passage graves of Northern Scotland, offer the following schemata:

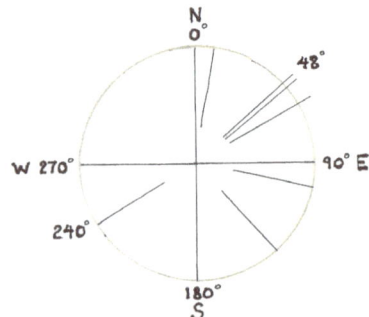
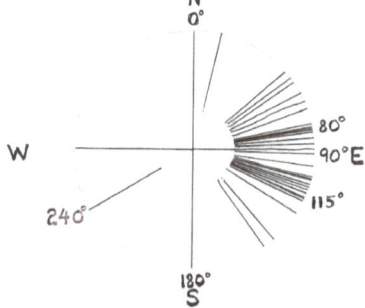
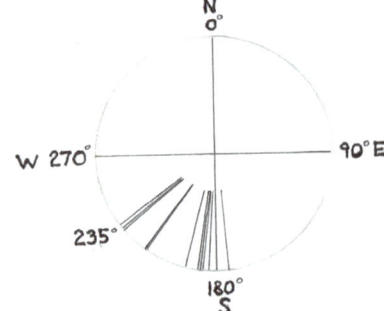

Figure 2. The axes of the long cairns of Northern Scotland (after Henshall and Ritchie)

Figure 3. The axes of chambers of Orkney-Cromarty Type tombs (after Henshall and Ritchie)

Figure 4. The axes of chambers of Clava type (after Henshall and Ritchie)

A recent study of the Barnhouse Settlement in Orkney (Richards, et al, 2005) shows that the hearth orientations of Late Neolithic houses appear to be evenly divided amongst the four quadrants around the solstices and lunar standstills, avoiding the quadrants of the four cardinal points of the compass by 25° or so, e.g. no orientation of a hearth between NE by E to E by S, according to the mariner's compass.

Other studies (Childe, Parker-Pearson, Richards, Hodder, Garnham, and others) have emphasized the importance of the orientation of the houses, and of the hearths in particular, as the centering point of the interior, and have shown the tendency of orientations in certain areas of the Isles to cluster around particular quadrants of the horizon.

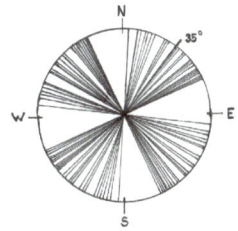

Figure 5. Late Neolithic hearth orientations in northern Britain, with 35° as the summer solstice rise (after Downes and Richards)

The one generalization that we thought could be made about these orientations, including those from the Upper Face at Achnabreck, is that some tomb types (and radial cuts of the cup and ring carvings), as well as houses, do tend to group their orientations within a certain quadrant and that some other quadrants appear to be generally avoided. We also speculated that the macehead would have been the most useful tool for achieving accuracy in orientation.

How many more correlations can be made between the cups and the tombs and the hearths and standing stones down in the Kilmartin Valley? Our next Scotland Tour may have the task of discovering the azimuths of the cups and rings of the other faces of carved rock at Achnabreck, as well as at Kilmichael Glassery and other sites nearby, and then of correlating them with the orientations of houses, hearths, and ceremonial sites in the surrounding valleys.

A section of the Upper Face at Achnabreck

17

Cup marked lid for a child's cist grave at Nether Largie South, Kilmartin. The grave is below ground level in the center of the tomb, and the lid has been removed and set on its side so that the visitor can observe the cup marks. According to our theory, the lid was used first as the basis for the orientation of the tomb as it was being laid out on the surface or the ground.

[Some archeologists, Norris and others, have been skeptical of generalizations concerning orientations or any deliberate alignments during our period, some even claiming that there are just too many possible sightlines for there to be anything other than a maze of lines, signifying nothing. However, because sightlines are chosen by the observer, based on the context of surrounding cairns, henges, standing stones, and the lunar and solar events observable from those points of view, and because we discover at some complex sites that certain orientations may have two or three sets of parallel lines, as we shall see at Maeshowe, they must have signified something more than nothing.]

More study will be done on the correlations noted in Figures 1-5. Scrutiny of the patterns shown above reveals that at the least, there must have been a keen interest in the calendar amongst the people of the area, in record keeping, and in orienting themselves and their dead with the risings and settings of the sun and moon: the orientations of all the major monuments, Maeshowe, Clava Cairns, Stonehenge, Newgrange, Callanish and others, face a solstice or major standstill or the equinox. And it would also seem as if there was an understanding amongst the leaders and engineers that the second tier monuments would avoid the cardinal orientations, instead, spreading their orientations evenly about the horizons. Perhaps it would have been presumptuous as well as silly for a small, isolated community to orient to a major standstill. Then they'd have missed the hoopla!

The Corrimony Cairn

The next day, the Scotland Tour IV made a fast trip from Kilmartin to Thurso, at the northernmost point in mainland Scotland, departing Oban at 8 am, and arriving at the Orkney Ferry by 6 pm. A fast coach north in ten hours, and yet with time to pack in three important side trips. First, a quick look at the slime green Loch Ness Monster moving slowly and silently through the pond next the hotel parking lot, and then a trip through the rolling hills up Urquhart territory to the Corrimony Cairn, which was after 4,000 years still sitting at the edge of a pasture bounded by forest opposite and a brook running past along the roadside. At around noon, two tripods were set up at the cairn, one on the floor of the center of the chamber where the cup-marked stone (now resting atop the wall of the cairn) would have been lying, the primary backsight benchmark, and a second tripod, set up some ten "megalithic" yards beyond the entrance, but centered in the middle of the passageway.

The Corrimony foresight, seen from the southwest

The Corrimony backsight, with stone marker and compass

As junior Ryan Trafton looked intently through the macehead, and lined up the two plumb strings, he got a very close reading of the point of the horizon where the winter sun would have dipped out of sight around the 21st of December, an orientation discussed by Richards in *The Good Stones*.

Next, we tried to imagine the empty pasture and to envision the process by which the cairn would have been oriented and its foundation laid out. We determined the point on the distant horizon where the strings merge to be the point of a notable rise or set. That alignment would make two dates on the calendar fairly accurate, the winter solstice sunset and the summer solstice sunrise, with the other cardinal dates worked out from that. Such accuracy and predictability, as a consequence, would have enhanced the authority of the clan leader and her chief engineer.

At Corrimony we speculated that the cup-marked slab lying on top of and next to the edge of the wall, which was likely the capstone of the chamber, as in the cist grave mentioned earlier, would have been first used for the layout of the cairn and would have been at the center of the floor of the interior as the cairn was being laid out. Then, once it had served its function as the bench mark for the layout of the whole operation, including orienting the circle of some twelve standing stones just inside the henge, it was moved outside the perimeter as the kerbstones were laid, the walls raised and the corbelled roof brought to a close, and was finally hoisted to the top of the cairn to be used as the capstone at the peak of the roof. One writer on Corrimony says it is likely that this cup-marked capstone was turned to face inwards, at the top of the ceiling, where the cup marks would be visible to those below.

> [As Eogan has amply demonstrated (1984, 1998) amongst the hundreds of carvings visible in passages and chambers, a number of decorated stones have also been found at Newgrange and Knowth reversed, and some clearly recycled, invisible to those in the passage, and that is the case with other tombs as well.]

The passageway into Corrimony is low enough to require entry on hands and knees. As some writers have suggested, this may be the reason for the constriction of the passages at three to four feet high on average—to inculcate an attitude of humility before emerging in the Room of the Bones, the Gate to the Otherworld of the Ancestors. And it was a humbling moment for us to enter these places of such sanctity and antiquity, all of us bending and creeping across the muddy stones, and remembering, when we could, to pay homage to the builders and the spirits of the dead.

The Corrimony backsight cord, seen from the center of the chamber

Corrimony is a quiet place, just next to a minor road and a stream. The cairn looks out down the pasture into the trees beyond. We tried to imagine the scene four or five thousand years ago—wind-swept and bare, a few miserable sheep foraging between the rocks, and a perfectly smooth horizon, ideal for catching the last rays of the sun. Pulled back to the present by hunger and thirst, we dismantled our tripods—this time no sticks but eighteen pieces of 28" pvc pipe and their couplers, three to a pole—and clambered back onto the coach.

The Clava Cairns

The third and last detour before the straight shot from near Inverness to Thurso: the Balanuran of Clava Cairns near the site of the Battle of Culloden in 1745. We passed this most famous Scottish battlefield, with the whole Motley Crew asleep, nodding in unison to the rhythm of the coach. But within two minutes these same nine nodding students popped right out of the coach again and grabbed up the tripods and maceheads, to check the sightings of the three Clava Cairns: The Northeastern Passage Cairn, the Middle Ring Cairn, and the Southwestern Passage Cairn.

The Middle Ring Cairn at Balanuran Clava seen from the Southwestern Passage Cairn, with the Northeastern Passage Cairn in the distance

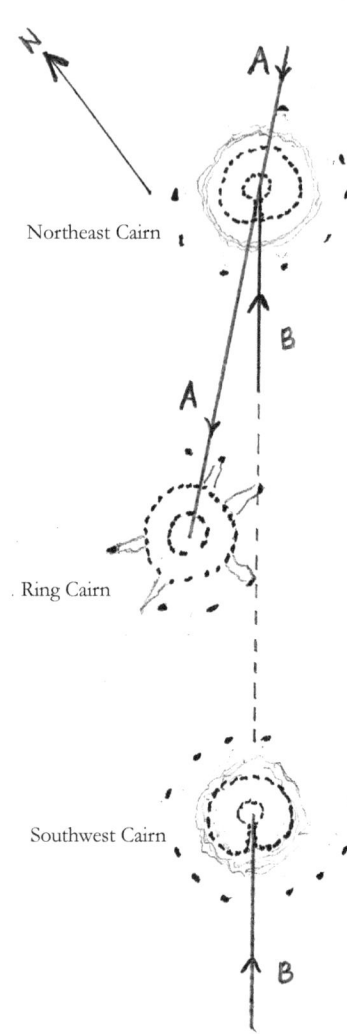

The three major cairns at Balnuran of Clava (after Bradley 2000)

Tour IV envisioned the precision of the orientations, both the NE Cairn's passage opening directly at the midwinter solstice sunset, and likewise the SW's passage orientation: the setting at the winter solstice in the southwest. The Ring Cairn's center point (the lower A in the diagram), as Bradley points out in *The Good Stones*, is offset so that the rising sun at midsummer, having to surmount the hills beyond, lines up with the NE Cairn's center point (the upper A), but not the center point of the SW Cairn.

Looking from the center of the NE Cairn over the edge across to the Ring Cairn, and then to the SW Cairn just to the left, we observe that the Ring Cairn is slightly offset to the west. At a point directly behind the observer, on the A line, the sun rises on the summer solstice. At the laying out of the Ring Cairn and the NE Cairn, the center point of the Ring Cairn was the backsight for the point at the center of the NE Cairn, which was the foresight of the summer solstice rise.

Thus the A line represents the rising summer solstice, which passes over the center of the NE Cairn and the center of the Ring Cairn. The Ring Cairn is offset so as not to block the primary orientation of the NE and SW Cairns, which is the solstice setting at azimuth 215° and to make the alignment with the NE Cairn and the summer solstice rise. The B line shows the direction of the winter solstice setting.

From the center of the NE Cairn (along the B line of the figure), and turning and facing the southwest, we can see the very practical use of the center of the NE Cairn as the backsight for the foresight at the center of the SW Cairn. Of course, there could have been several other ways to determine the spacing and orientation of the three cairns. We will see the same bases for the orientations of the monuments around the Ring of Brodgar and Stonehenge: the meeting of two lines of orientation at a point, their relation to the north-south line, and the pattern of angles that emerges on the ground. If we imagine an open space, with tripods and maceheads and carved balls, this all could have been set up in a jiffy and modified in a few seconds, while the astronomer, sighting through the macehead and tripod, cords, and carved balls, gives instruction to her mates, as the sun sets on one of the three shortest days of the year, or rises on one of the three longest days of the year.

The Northeast Clava Cairn without its roof

The left portal stone with cupmarks

Before the Northeast Clava Cairn was begun, as was likely the case with the Corrimony Cairn capstone, one can imagine that the cup-marked stone used to set the point of the foresight, with the backsight at the center of the chamber, was then, upon the building of the foundation, set in the place of honor: the left doorpost as one enters the chamber.

[Several of the standing stones that encircle the tombs have cupmarks. They would have been prone while in use as backsights or foresights, but then raised upon completion of the monument, subsequently serving as foresights for other alignments sighted from the center of the tombs. The orthostats and the platforms found radiating from the Central Ring Cairn can be seen as setting orientations with the solar cardinal points, including the north-south line. Another issue related to that of alignments is that of the coloration of the stones, the black and red from the interior foundation stones matching the red and black stones used in the exterior circle. Analysis and discussion is found in Bradley, *The Good Stones*. Stevenson also discusses the common practice of moving stones for reuse in the fabric of the building.]

Such accuracy of orientation, we thought, could have been accomplished with just the sort of "sophisticated" tools we have described above, although writers on the subject of alignments assert the inability of these farmers to make much more than a rough approximation of an alignment. We noted the similarity of the ground plan of the passage and ring cairns with the cup and ring marks: the bare cup with one or more rings mimicking the Ring Cairn, and the cup and ring with radial cut, the Passage Cairns. One student noted quietly, "Wow! The cup and ring carvings we saw are a replication of the shape of these cairns. . ." This similarity has been noted by a number of writers, and the carvers themselves must have seen the carvings as replications, especially since they oriented their major tombs and their principal houses to the cardinal points on the lunar and the solar risings and settings and built them in the same general shape as the cup and ring carvings.

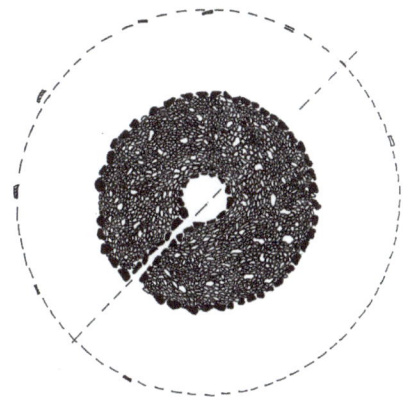

Diagram of Southwest Clava Cairn Passage grave at Balauran of Clava (Hana Kurniawati)

The NE Clava Cairn, the viewer looking past the orthostats of the remaining stone circle, directly into the entrance of the cairn, which opens to the southwest, the setting sun at the winter solstice. The cup-marked orthostat on the right when aligned with the center of the NE Cairn yields the north-south line.

After we noted once more the cup marks on the left portal stone of the NW passage cairn as well as those cupmarks on the standing stones nearby, we dismantled the eighteen pieces of the tripods, the cords, and the two maceheads, stowed them all away in the overhead, and settled in for the magnificent spectacle of the eastern coast of Scotland and the North Sea from the new road, fortunately with fewer "Beware Oncoming Vehicles in Middle of Roadway" signs and less thrillingly treacherous switch-back curves. But for this jet-lagged Scotland Crew IV, orienting a 5,000 year old cairn is very hard work, so sleep was the order at the end of the day—heads all nodding in unison into the dark. And after a smooth passage through the Pentwirth Straits aboard the sleek new *MS Hamnavoe* ferry, we checked into the Kirkwall Orkney youth hostel for our first really good night's sleep in Scotland.

Kerbstone at the SW Clava Cairn with cupmarks and cup and ring

THE ORKNEYS

The Stones of Stennis from the Ring of Brodgar

The four days in the Orkneys gave us the obligatory tourists' (as well as student archeologists' field trip) glimpses of several important monuments: We looked in at Unstan, for its perfect stone masonry and for its being the eponymous find site of the Unstan class of pottery; at Cuween Hill, for the tomb of the 24 dogs heads' totem and for the view to Wideford Hill Tomb directly across the valley; at Wideford Hill Tomb and its concentric walls of stone and for its orientation directly toward the tomb at Cuween Hill; and at Isbister, Tomb of the Eagles, for the sleet, the sea, and the cliffs, but most of all for the superb lectures given to visitors of the Museum at the Tomb of the Eagles by Katherine and Freda, the daughters of Ronald Simison, the discoverer and excavator of the tomb and the Bronze Age house nearby. The Tour was grateful to the curators for allowing them to actually handle the 5,000 year old skull of a former resident of the tomb, as well as permitting the testing of the glass-smooth surface of the polished macehead found by Ronald Simison at the northeast corner of the outer wall of the Tomb, just above the cliffs and the wide expanse of the North Sea. And we had wicked fun with granny's skateboard out at the Tomb of the Eagles. Sliding in and out. In and out. We took note of the orientation of the passage of the tomb, as well as the configurations of the side chambers within. The orientation of the passageway of the tomb, as John Hedges and others have observed, is set for the few days in April and again in August, when the rising sun is coming up just to the north of due east. One might say at northeast by east. The sun is moving north in April (or south in early August) just a few days after equinox (or before). So with such a stupendous view over the sea to the east, why not orient the tomb to some cardinal orientation, like the equinox? Perhaps the reason was, as noted earlier, that there was amongst the clan leaders an understanding that only the great ritual centers could appropriate the cardinal points. The Isbister people would not have oriented the Tomb of the Eagles to the summer solstice. They deferred to the people at Barnhouse and Skara Brae. And after all, had they been so presumptuous as to set their own orientation to the solstice, then they would have been more likely to miss the big late June solstice celebration at the Ring of Brodgar. So for a few days twice a year the people of Isbister had their own celebration, and what a solemn moment it must have been when the full force of the sun shone directly into the darkness of the chamber for a few long minutes on those three or four days. A flood of sunlight blasting into the chambers of the dead.

[On the matter of ritual celebrated at the tombs, and with particular reference to Ireland, Williams and Pearce have summarized their view concerning which segments of the population would be admitted to what part of the ritual space: "At Knowth, Newgrange and other tombs, a few crossed the image-embellished kerb and entered the passage; perhaps some stopped in the passage, alerted by specially placed imagery or other features; a few went on in to the actual chamber, while others stood on the flat summit of the mound. Outside the tombs, especially those that have forecourts, there were probably other distinctions marked off by distance from the centre of the tomb. Many researchers recognize this social function of Neolithic monuments. We add that control of altered states of consciousness and parallels with the structure of the cosmos went hand in hand with those distinctions. Cosmos and consciousness underwrote social discrimination. Power resided in [the] control of consciousness and transition through the cosmos, and was epitomized by megalithic monuments" (Williams and Pearce 248).]

On another day of hiking, we climbed up Cuween Hill a few hundred yards above the car park, and later Wideford Hill Tomb after a long slog through the mud and the heather. As we began to contemplate the situation at Wideford and Cuween Hill Tombs, facing each other across the valley, one due east (Cuween Hill) and the other due west, we realized that they would have experienced the equinox on the same day, the sun flashing down the passages to the end, first at Cuween at the sunrise, and then Wideford at the sunset a half day later. On the day of the equinox the Wideford people would have felt the frisson of the blast of the full sun in the center of the tomb at sundown. And furthermore, the flood of light would have revealed several

Cuween Hill Tomb from the northeast. This magnificent little chambered tomb is set into the hillside and contains several side chambers, just large enough for small people to wiggle into and to stand up in. Its very low passageway faces the rising sun at due east, the equinox.

Student entering chamber to commune with the spirits of the ancestors...

incisions in the stone on the facing wall, only recently discovered by Richard Bradley and his colleagues (2002), which incisions are very like motifs found elsewhere in Orkney, particularly on the Large Orkney Stone, as we shall soon see. For Scotland IV, orientations were beginning to be meaningful and significant, and not just esoteric and abstract.

The physical opposition of Cuween and Wideford opens another avenue of speculation. Since one factor in the setting of alignments and orientations is the lightness and portability of the macehead and tripod, the rig could be moved easily to another location twenty miles away in one day to make the same sorts of alignments for another family or clan. And it would follow that, in the same manner, with these tools, the ritual calendar could have been maintained and cross-checked throughout the lands. The people at Newgrange (midwinter sunrise) would have known precisely when the celebrations would be happening at Stonehenge and Maeshowe (midwinter sunset). The solstice sunrise shone through the roofbox at Newgrange around our December 21, on the same day as the sun would set between the sarsens of the middle trilithon of the famous horseshoe at Stonehenge. Likewise, at the primary orientation of Stonehenge, the midsummer sunrise would have occurred on the same day as the midsummer setting at the Ring of Brodgar at its primary orientation toward the northwest. Neolithic people, especially the shaman-priest-elder-astronomer-engineer, must have been very well aware of what was going on, ritually, at the major monuments thoughout the Isles.

Moreover, when we consider the mix of artifacts of stone and clay and flint from everywhere to everywhere in the Isles, and the communication which that implies between many widely separated locations, judging from the remaining physical evidence, we should not be surprised that our Neolithic period evinces widespread trade and sharing of artifacts, burial traditions, and monument traditions, as Bradley and Chapman have shown. It is often said, the sea was the highway, not the barrier. On the issue of portability of objects Mary Helms concludes that "portability, as a feature of materiality and tangibility, obviously makes cosmological qualities literally attainable in that portable objects can literally transmit a portion of the cosmic world directly into the house or community, where their energizing qualities can be put to use" (Helms 125). The macehead was an artifact that united all the important features of their universe: the earth and rock and stone, the horizon, the sun and moon, the orientation of their buildings, and the eye of the observer. It had become, in D. V. Clarke's phrase, a symbol of power. No doubt the people from Skara Brae, Barnhouse, Isbister, Cuween Hill, and all the rest of the estimated seventy-six Orkney clans would gather for the high feast days, and very likely there would have been visitors from other lands and peoples present, a visiting dignitary from Avebury perhaps, or from Loughcrew, exchanging pots, polished knives, balls, and maceheads, and carrying messages from afar to the locals on the islands. One analogy to the traveling wise one from earliest Anglo-Saxon times is the 8th century poem of the scop Widsith, who has travelled throughout the world, entertained many tribes and kings, and always received gold rings from those "learned in song and the weaving of words." We may also wonder what sort of poetic and musical traditions would have been found amongst our Neolithic forebears.

The Village of Skara Brae

On our visit to Skara Brae the next day, walking around the edges of the walls and peering into the living rooms and sleeping quarters, we got some idea of the locations of the bedstead carvings, and of the findspots of some of the carved balls with knobs (Houses 3 and 7: Childe 1950) and cup and ring balls, not to mention, the Large Orkney Stone, the huge, flat "mystery stone" excavated from the midden by D. V. Clarke in 1973. This village is only one of several fairly well-preserved in Orkney, but more than any other, Skara Brae is a time capsule, yielding more information, both broad and deep, than any other site. The Orkney Islands themselves, somewhat remote from the more rapid changes taking place during the Bronze and Iron Ages, is in many ways a laboratory of the Neolithic, with perhaps more artifacts and monuments per square mile than anywhere in Britain. We will study the artifacts themselves later in the week at the National Museums of Scotland.

House 2: Bedsteads on right and left, hearth in the center, the clay-lined stone containers, grinding quern, and the central "dresser." The flat tops of these bedsteads contain many incisions.

Life-size replica of a Skara Brae House with stone furniture

Bedstead at the replica of a Skara Brae House

The bedsteads at Skara Brae House 2

The Large Orkney Stone, found at Skara Brae (NMS)

The passageways at Skara Brae. The Atlantic Ocean, having once been 200 yards from the village, has partially eroded the passageways and houses, which are now protected by a bulkhead.

Speculating at the Ring of Brodgar

But for now, moving from Skara Brae to the Ring of Brodgar at the heart of Orkney, we were able to find tentative confirmation of the feasibility of the use of macehead, tripod, benchmark, and stake. Standing in the complex of the Isthmus of Stennis on a chilly, overcast day, with the carvings of the stones of Skara Brae in the backs of our mind, we seem to be in another world, as Gordon Childe suggested early on about Skara Brae: a world of astronomers and engineers, specialists in the lunar and solar risings and settings, in the correlations of the orientation of the circles, tombs, henges, and houses. They were the power people, who alone possessed the tools to accomplish the building of these great works.

On the evening of April 17, we set up a tripod on Salt Knowe, and we sighted through the macehead to the notch on the Hill of Hellias, just where the moon would be at the major southwest standstill. Next we moved the tripods and set them up once again, the first one at the center of the Ring, and the other 30 feet towards the southwest to align with the same point at Hellias. The sun was past the equinox, and it was about 8:30 pm.

If we had been here 5,000 years ago, we would have sighted through the two tripods and cords to that point on the hills, and we would have found a way to memorize the alignment and orientation of the point at the notch at Hellias where the moon made its southernmost setting every 18.6 years.

After making our alignments, we observed that the primary orientation of the Ring itself and the henge is the northwest, at the summer solstice sunset. We speculated that at the laying out of the Ring, the first base line established would be the north-south line. It would seem reasonable that when setting up the dimensions of any Neolithic building, a north-south line would be set first, by lining up the tools with the North Star—using maceheads, stone weights, and carved stone balls as benchmarks, and cords and tripods—and then by setting out a line on the ground between the benchmarks. That line would be absolute north-south as far as their eyes could tell,

View through two cords at the Ring of Brodgar in Orkney

and from that line could easily be determined the east-west orientation using the 3-4-5 right triangle, very like the one incised on the Large Orkney Stone. At the Ring of Brodgar, the alignments, suggested by Thom and corroborated by MacKie and others, result from lines drawn from the center of the Ring outward (as does the Northwest Bridge across the henge, opening out in the direction of the summer solstice setting, with the other three alignments pointing to lunar standstills).

[Shifting the viewpoint towards another aspect of our experimentation and speculation, we find that the noonday sun, and hence the meridian or north-south line, can be determined on any given day within a month either side of the solstices when there is full sun visible at the rising and the setting. Against a flat horizon from one backsight the morning rise foresight is marked and a twenty foot cord is stretched along that alignment. Then at the setting, the same backsight is used to align the sunset and the twenty foot cord is stretched along that alignment. This yields an angle with two equal sides. Pulling a cord of whatever length is needed between the two foresights at the end of each angle, and then halving the length, yields at that midpoint the foresight of the north-south line from the original backsight. That north-south line should make a right angle with "the cord of whatever length." Observations closer to the times around the winter solstice would yield a more equilateral triangle, with the observer looking south, or around the summer solstice, looking north; the times around the equinox would yield a more obtuse triangle with a much elongated hypotenuse and more chance of error, all of these speculations subject to some inaccuracies, depending on the altitude of the horizon and hence the declination of the sun or moon.]

MacKie and Thom have also observed alignments between several points that do not pass through the center of the Ring. Perhaps these points were marked in the early years of the use of the Ring, and the points made monumental by a later generation through the building of cairns. Most of the alignments between cairns have one or two other parallel alignments.

A sighting from the center of the Ring of Brodgar, past the second tripod to the notch in the distant Hill of Helias

[The dozens of other random sightings over any and all of the possible alignments are omitted on principle, as we noted earlier. The argument that, because there are so very many possible sightlines, the whole concept of sightlines as anciently derived from stone circles must be thrown out of the discussion—that argument is, we would argue, defunct. For example, Stonehenge is, amongst its many other uses, unquestionably a monument oriented to the summer and winter solstices. Newgrange is a monument oriented to the winter solstice rising. Maeshowe to the winter solstice set. Callanish to the equinox. Study of the sun and moon, and the use of that study in the disposition of buildings, customs and rituals, and setting up alignments with the sun and moon and points on the earth, was the first order of importance for these people. Of course, our setting up the tripods at the Ring of Brodgar and getting alignments across the horizon proved nothing at all, except that it was feasible to discover and certify orientations this way, using only Neolithic tools.]

Barnhouse is the remains of several dwellings only a few hundred yards from both Maeshowe and the Ring of Brodgar. In the superb report of the excavation at Barnhouse, directed by Colin Richards, and carried out by a team of experts in virtually every department of archeological analysis, Richards paints a picture of Orkney in broad strokes, based on the enormous quantity of evidence unearthed at the site: "What was it like to have inhabited a Neolithic Orcadian world where the forces of nature featured so strongly in life and death? The long daylight of summer and the darkness of winter, the terrific storms which turned the sea into a dangerous and hostile entity and the winds which scoured the land provided the conditions under which people lived their lives. It was also a world where the dead were ever present in one form or another and watched over the living. It is this alien world that provides the object of this study . . ." (Richards 22). Our study, however superficial, attempts to speculate as to how that Neolithic world dealt with their days and nights, incorporating this knowledge into the physical ordering of the world around them.

Speculating at the Ring of Brodgar with the 3-4-5 Pythagorean triangle

At this point in the trip, our last day before leaving Orkney, we had seen the maceheads and carved stones at the Kilmartin Museum, had seen the same at the Tankerness House Museum in Kirkwall, Orkney, but we hadn't seen the many maceheads and other decorated stones discovered from other areas of Scotland, nor had we seen the actual bedsteads from Skara Brae. And there was one other stone carving of which we had only seen pictures: the Large Orkney "Mystery Stone," excavated by Clarke from the midden at Skara Brae, and now enjoying a life of retirement and ease in the Early People gallery of the National Museums Scotland.

So the Scotland Tour IV made a fast trip from the Orkney Youth Hostel with a smooth sail on the beautiful stainless steel and glass *MS Hamnavoe*, a drive down along the North Sea again to St. Andrew's golf course, past the University of St. Andrew's Department of Logic and Metaphysics and the ruins of the once formidable Cathedral of St. Andrew, and so on to Edinburgh at last, to the National Museums Scotland.

Speculating through the backsight macehead across the Loch of Stennis

National Museums Scotland

Standing in one section of the Early People gallery of the Museums, one still seems to be positively surrounded by artifacts from Orkney, not the houses and the standing stones, but the portable ones. And there are representative samples of stone objects from all over Scotland as well: several maceheads, polished knives, jet buttons, bone awls, and carved balls. In addition to the portable objects, we observed the large stones from Eday Manse, Orkney, with its two cups and rings and horned double spiral and the very Pierowall Quarry stone, Westray Orkney, with their deeply incised "Boyne Valley" motifs. So when we recalled their likely source in Newgrange and the many other important Irish sites, and in view of the thousands of cup and rings, especially in the north of Britain, we realized that there are virtually no cup and ring carvings in the Orkneys. They are found in profusion nearly everywhere else in Britain, especially Aberdeenshire, but not in Orkney, except on the Eday Stone and the Pierowall Quarry Stone.

The Eday Manse Stone (NMS)

The Pierowall Quarry Stone (Orkney Museum, now removed to Pierowall)

But this realization leads to another puzzle: With no cupmarks carved in stone outcroppings, what did the Orkney people do to mark their backsights? They needed a backsight, a point on the ground, over which the macehead is to be centered. The point should be tamper-proof, as it were. An immoveable stone would do best, a flat outcrop like Achnabreck. (Back at school in Maine, with tripods and maceheads set up in our classroom, we had used a 15-pound chunk of white quartz and a laser pointer up and down at an angle of about 50° on the far wall for a sun.) By analogy, it seemed reasonable to us that the Orkney astronomers wanted a stone that was visible from twenty yards or so away, even one that showed craftsmanship and beauty, a stone that perhaps only the engineer had the right to handle, and so, we speculated, the "mystery" stone, the carved ball, came to be, intended to be used as either a benchmark on the ground or as the plumb bob of the second tripod.

A generic six-knobbed carved ball (NMS). The Museum's collection includes dozens of carved balls, virtually identical to this one on display. It is as if there was a special factory/workshop (e.g. House 8, Skara Brae) for the replication of this basic form. They may have been turned out one after the other, using a sort of jig, such as a V-notch in a slab of sandstone. They were perhaps then distributed via the shamans throughout the Isles for the setting of the cord of the backsight.

Dorothy N. Marshall (1973) and Graham and Anna Ritchie (1991) found that some 390 carved stone balls have survived, scattered throughout Britain, with concentrations in Aberdeenshire. Virtually all show signs of high craftsmanship and, of course, should be regarded as rock *art*. But we speculated that the primary function of the carved ball was not to exhibit art for art's sake, mere decoration as some would have it, but that it should be hung from a cord and used as a plumb bob, or on the other hand, placed on the ground, to mark a fixed point during the setting out of the monument. The carved ball is therefore primarily a tool, made beautiful to fit with the undoubted solemnity of the occasion of its use. Marshall has found some 173 balls with six knobs and a few others with higher numbers of knobs. Knobs and other geometrical devices carved into the stone ball would have made each unique to its owner, as well as being more easily wrapped by a thong or cradle and hung from the center of the tripod. The several balls decorated with cup and ring, like those found at Skara Brae, could certainly have served as the ground benchmark stone in many areas without stone outcrops, and the more plainly carved balls certainly could have been used as the plumb bob of the second tripod.

Varieties of carved balls. These specimens are rather unusual, compared to the lack of variety of the products of the "factory."

Indeed, another new theory has been offered concerning the meaning and use of the Neolithic artistic motifs. If Jeremy Dronfield's theory of the association of the spiral, lattice, and the shaman is tenable, then the spirals on the balls from the Orkneys, and from Kilmartin and over to Newgrange, as well as the walls of many tombs, would have merged the practice of the shaman with that of the astronomer. The spirals would signify common ground between the astronomer and the shaman. The astronomer knows the sun and the moon and thus sets the calendar and the Days of Ritual. The celebrations are then enacted by the shaman with the assistance of the lattices and spirals, the "membranes," (to borrow Dronfield's word), through which the shaman passes on the journey to the Land of the Dead. Many have remarked on the double or triple roles played by the clan leader—wise one, shaman, priest, astronomer—in one clansperson. For example, the unique Towie Stone, with its clear association with the spirals of Kerbstone 1 and Kerbstone 52 of Newgrange and its potential use as a plumb bob, would perhaps have been the property of and regalia of the "arch-shaman," as it were, the one who perhaps had taught the science to the folk around Towie in Aberdeenshire and who died there with his beautiful carved stone, which had been passed down a long line of astronomer-shamans until it rested with its final owner. With the sole exception of the Knowth macehead, the Towie Stone is the finest in the land. A brilliant work of craftsmanship in any age.

The Towie Stone (NMS)

Besides the carved balls, there are two other types of carved stones from Skara Brae, now at National Museums Scotland in Edinburgh—one, the so-called "phallic stone," or short stake, and the other, the so-called "stone object," shaped like a T-handle.

Three knobbed balls and two stone stakes from Skara Brae (NMS)

The first, we theorize, while it may have a phallic shape, would have been the perfect field marker around which to pull a cord: Set up the first tripod, drop the macehead, mark the backsight point on the ground with the "object" or "short stake." Jam it into the soil. Tie the cord to it and run the cord to the mark in the distance where a second stone or stake would serve to mark the point on the ground from whence the next sighting would be made. The design of the stone stake is perfect for the purpose: one end pointed; the other, a perfectly shaped handle for gripping. (A wooden stake 203 mm. long, carved similarly, but broken, was also uncovered at Skara Brae, as noted by Clarke and Sharples. The wood was spruce and had floated from somewhere along the coast of present-day Canada to the Orkneys.)

The second "stone object"—the T-handle—has carvings of fine precision across the top: the upper half of Lozenge I (of the Large Orkney Stone), several angles of orientation, each in its own little compartment, as it were, and a checkerboard of 35 perfect squares. If this object were used as a guide to the orientations required, the "handle" could be pushed into the soil, the ends pointing along the north to south line, and then the angles of orientation could be read from the carvings on the top and sides. It would have been a useful tool in the training of their young people, whether it was pushed into the ground at the center of the Ring or its incisions handled and studied by the novice, as so many youngsters may have done before in the furs and fleeces of the warm semi-darkness of House Seven on a winter's night in the late third millenium BC.

The Skara Brae T-handle (NMS)

The incisions across the top of the T-handle mimic the incisions of the lozenges of the Large Orkney Stone

The bedstead carvings at Skara Brae: lines of orientation

In another museum case we find more stone carvings. If we take a closer look at the carvings on one bedstead slab from House 7 at Skara Brae, we see deep cuts across the slab at the end. Then, two or three triangles and other deep cuts along the slab, including several of the only curved incisions found in the Orkney corpus. (Curves are difficult to incise. It is for the same reason that the Anglo-Saxon runes are all straight lines and angles when carved on stone or ivory or iron.)

Bedstead of House 7 in the village of Skara Brae, with its incisions (Crown copyright: reproduced courtesy of Historic Scotland)

Details of Bedstead of House 7 showing similarities to the lozenges of the Large Orkney Stone.

If a vertical line, one going across the narrow edge of the slab, represents one line of sight, say the north-south alignment, then the oblique line could represent the solstice or other point of a particular orientation. This is precisely replicated on K74 at Knowth (see p. 40), where a wide vertical cut bisects the stone and lines up east and west, with the rising and setting of the equinox sun and the orientations of both passageways. A second line, carved with sharp edges shoots off to the southeast, just like the verticals and the offshoots on the tops of the Skara Brae bedsteads. Although archeologists assert that the line is a natural incision, the author has personally observed that that straightness of the cut and its precise depth more likely show the work of the human hand.

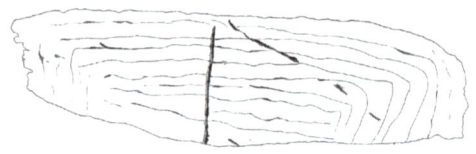

Kerbstone 74 at the entrance of the western tomb of Knowth passage tomb. The vertical line, like the one on the entrance stone K 1 at Newgrange, shows the primary orientation, which is east-west, the double passageways admitting light on the equinox. The nested curves may represent the path of the sun. The oblique incision, even more pronounced than the east-west one, marks out azimuth 210°, near the midwinter solstice set, in the Valley of the Boyne. (Photo: Kevin Champney. Drawing: Hana Kurniawati)

Although drawings in two studies of this stone do not even show this incision, it is clearly neither a flaw in the face nor a crack in the stone itself. As with the foundation stones at Clava Northeast Cairn, and with the capstone at Corrimony, once the stones had done their business, prone, of marking as a benchmark the backsight of the orientation, they were then incorporated into the fabric of the building. Stevenson has shown the ubiquity of this practice of reusing cup-marked stones. Furthermore, several writers (Ruggles, Brennan, Twohig, Burl and others) have seen the two most highly decorated stones from Knowth (SE4 and SW22, also incorporated into the fabric) as calendrical, marking off radiating lines as a sun-dial and as showing the phases of the moon through crescents, circles, and spirals.

The Knowth calendar stone, Kerbstone 15 shows the sightlines radiating from a central point: the cup. Any number of orientations could be extrapolated from these lines, depending of course, on the base line's indication—north-south or east-west or, less likely, one of the solstices or moon standstills. This stone and many other decorated stones functioned as a catechism, the stones passing down the rituals, the methods, and the secrets to the next generations.

At Loughcrew Cairn T, Ireland, near the Hag's Chair (Queen Maeve's throne), itself profusely covered with cup and ring, spiral, and lunar signs, we find a large kerbstone with several oblique parallel lines set at an angle to a primary incision. If the primary incision is the north-south line, the oblique lines would point to an important celestial event. They are analogous to the parallel lines of the large Orkney Stone.

Turning in the mind back to Orkney, we see that one of the Skara Brae bedsteads and the slab from the Ring of Brodgar are carved with several motifs that derive from the astronomy, and these motifs have, through repetition, mutated into the motifs typical of the pottery, especially those found on the Unstan bowls and on Grooved Ware shards. According to Barclay, these ceramic artifacts have been found in contexts where maceheads have also been discovered. Several other writers, including Burl and Brennan, have seen the nested chevrons and the zigzag motifs as representing the rising and setting of the sun. And in an article discussing the Mafa and Bulahay of northern Cameroon, "Why Pots are Decorated," authors David, Sterner, and Gavua write that "specific decorative motifs represent cosmological and religious concepts, and similar patterns of decoration of different pot types express coherent underlying perceptions, accounting for continuities in an "art" form in which no one is particularly interested." Dare one suggest that the same expressions of cosmological and religious concepts might be seen, by analogy, in the pots of the Neolithic people?

A Bronze Age beaker, decorated with lozenges, intersecting lozenges, and zigzags identical to those at K 52 Newgrange, and the slab from the Brodgar Farm (Cambridge Mueseum of Archaeology)

It is at this point that technology is given artistic expression: when the same motif is repeated, of sightlines, risings and settings of celestial bodies, lozenges and parallel lines, we find the nested chevrons and zigzag motifs.

Slab from the Brodgar Farm just a few hundred yards from the Ring of Brodgar and the Ring of Bookan: motifs from the practice of astronomical alignments applied to stone. From left to right, nested chevrons, zigzags, and subdivided lozenges. (NMS)

[We may be reminded that Caroline Malone has said, in the context of her discussion of the designs on the Folkton Drums: "The rock art consists of zigzags, concentric rings and cup marks, linear and geometric patterns of triangles. It is never naturalistic in Britain" (254).]

THE TRIPODS DEPICTED IN THE STONES?

As we focused on the bedsteads at the Museum in Edinburgh, a number of other carvings that seemed at first sight to be random scratchings, actually appeared to be depictions of *things of nature*, suggesting that they were making designs of things "out there," and this may imply that there are other levels of meaning than being merely decorative motifs or graffitti: The nested chevrons, for example, represent perfectly two tripods, one a few feet away.

In addition to what we believe to be the depictions of tripods as they would have been seen in the field, there is a palimpsest of countless triangles, any of which could have been part of the template used in the laying out of the monuments. Another deliberate similarity between elements of motifs is that the two parallel lines on either side of the nested major lozenge shapes (see below), standing as columns demarcating the nested lozenges from the rest of the surface, are the same as those "columns" on the Large Orkney Stone. But there is more.

Two views along the top of a bedstead at Skara Brae (NMS)

Tripods close up and far away, incised on the bedstead of House 7, with possible carved stone as plumb bob. Perhaps this was the scene at the Ring, when several tripods were set up at once to determine several orientations. It might have looked like a jungle out there. (NMS)

Naturalistic vistas on the bedsteads?

As evocative as these "random" scratchings are, the most astonishing carvings of all are found in the middle of the slab from House 7. This slab shows the only curved lines to be found on any of the bed slabs, and, when viewed one way, along the longer surface, seems to depict a seascape with two rounded hills in the distance, one half in front of the other, and two straight lines descending at the same angle of declination as the sun sets over the Loch of Stennis and the hills beyond near the time of the winter solstice.

A portion of the bedstead showing the flat surface of the loch, and above, two hills, depicted by curved incisions, one higher than the other, with two straight incisions above them, showing the angles of the sun and moon as they set over the hills beyond. (NMS)

View from the southeastern quadrant of the Ring of Brodgar, over the Comet Stone in the center of the photograph, to the hills beyond

A second image a few inches along the bedstead would seem to mirror the view from Brodgar, across the Loch of Stennis, to the Hills of Hoy, high in the far distance some 433 m at the summit of Cullags. This incision (opposite page) is the most deeply cut of all those on the bedstead and rather than having been carved by a sharp point of quartz, yielding a triangular incision as in all the others, appears to have been carved by a tiny flat chisel. The cut is over one eighth of an inch flat at the base and is deep, which makes this carving stand out from all the rest. Could these incisions be the first pictorial representations in prehistoric art since the Chauvet Cave paintings were made or such goddollies as the Venus of Willendorf were conceived several thousand years before the Neolithic Period?

View from the Ring of Brodgar across the Loch of Stennis to the Hills of Hoy in the distance

A portion of the bedstead with deep incisions (NMS)

Are there any other examples of naturalistic depiction anywhere in British or Irish Neolithic stone carving? Not to our knowledge. So, if not, the bedstead carvings would add one more piece of complexity to our understanding of the iconography of the Neolithics, and perhaps give us one small glimpse into the mind of our engineer, who arrogated to himself the right to depict here, and only here, a *naturalistic* representation in this view of the loch, the hills beyond, and the sky.

One can imagine a group of astronomers and engineers, five thousand years ago, moving back and forth between home and the ritual center at the Ring, bringing with them each time the tools of the trade, the tripods, the cords, the maceheads, and the "mystery" stones. That the inhabitants of Skara Brae and Barnhouse had an interest in astronomy is an understatement. They were obsessed with it! The Barnhouse Settlement excavation revealed a number of maceheads in various states of finish. The Skara Brae people were carving sightlines and triangles and parallel lines all over the tops of their bedsteads and along the passageways, and leaving maceheads, carved balls, and other unique stone artifacts, not to mention scatterings of quartz here and there throughout the houses. And when they did abandon their houses, it must have been in a mad flurry of activity! We can imagine the panic to get out that led to the scatter of beads found in the passageway where someone's necklace broke in the rush. No time even to pick up her most precious treasure. But for us the most important artifacts from the houses at Skara Brae are the carvings on the bedsteads and lintels, and the designs incised on the formidable Large Orkney Stone.

The Large Orkney Stone

The Large Orkney Stone with its four pointed lozenges (NMS)

I II III IV

The Large Orkney Stone discovered in D. V. Clarke's excavation is unique in its being one of the largest artifacts to come out of the Orkney Islands and in its deliberate precision of incisions, which have until now never been deconstructed or interpreted. We will designate the lozenges left to right as I, II, III, and IV. At the point where the lower left side of III makes a V-shape, we find what we will call the north-south line (in the figure opposite, Incision 1). Crossing it from an angle of approximately 42° is a second line (Incision 2 in the same figure), cut more deeply than the first. And a third line is incised from NW to SE. A close-up of the crossings reveals clearly the order in which the three lines were engraved: first, the north-south; second, the NE-SW line at 42°, and third, the NW-SE line at about 345°.

Furthermore, in the upper quadrant of the right side of Lozenge III, just to the right of the six parallel lines, we find a line carved perpendicular to the north-south line and cut rather deeply into the stone. This is the only incision that is out of parallel with all the other lines. It has no parallel partner. This unique cut is set at an exact 90° to the north-south line, pointing precisely to the equinox sunrise and sunset. The east-west line is carefully engraved, stopping right at the middle of the third and fourth parallel cuts that divide the upper triangle of III.

The hypotenuse of the triangle is the 42° line, and the triangle is a Pythagorean 3-4-5. Why there should be six diagonal cuts in the upper part of III, parallel to the three cuts in the lower part of III, is an enigma, but at the very least shows understanding of measurement and proportionality. And there are other features that cry out for explanation, such as the rather imprecise scratchings on II and IV, which seem to be intended to replicate the crossings of III, and the seemingly random triangles, such as the one at the lowest part of Lozenge I.

Pythagorean Triangle next to upper section of lozenge III

Incision 1
Incision 2
Incision 3

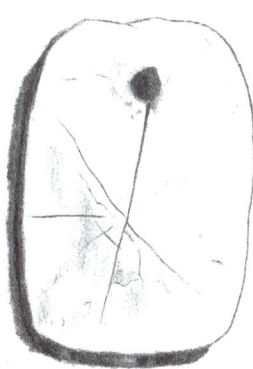

An amulet from Skara Brae, showing the angles of orientation similar to the crossings on the Large Orkney Stone. (Hana Kurniawati)

Closeup of the crossings at the foot of lozenge III

As we have noted earlier, if one applies this theory of the carving of that stone to the purported sightlines of the Ring of Brodgar, the outlying cairns, and the orientations of the entrances to the Ring, there appears to be a reasonable fit.

The Large Orkney Stone could therefore be thought of as a kind of visual catechism to teach the young the mysteries of the heavens and the layout of the monuments, as well as to serve as a mnemonic and iconic device through the hundreds of years during which these monuments and houses served as a focus of life for the Orkney clans.

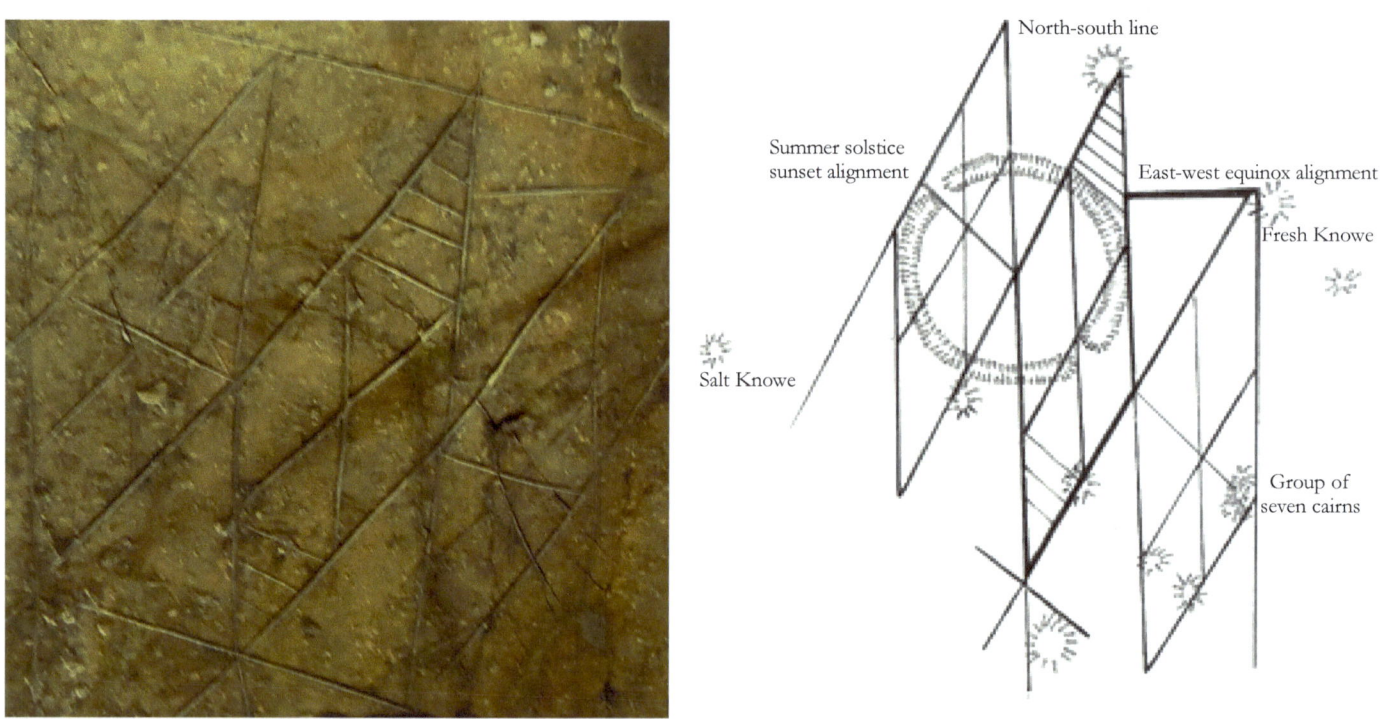

Closeup of the Large Orkney Stone (left). The major celestial alignments at the Ring of Brodgar, based on Thom and McKie (right). The diagram shows the pattern of the Large Orkney Stone superimposed upon the major sightlines of the Ring of Brodgar. The six parallel lines of the upper half of the Large Orkney Stone match the proportional distance from the center of the ring to the ditch and the ditch to Fresh Knowe.

Back to the Ring of Brodgar

Using the Large Orkney Stone as the template for the Ring of Brodgar, we tried to determine how the Neolithics, starting from scratch on a level field at, for example, Brodgar, would have laid out the orientations and in what order. Just as we had speculated earlier in the week at Corrimony Cairn, we decided that, since the Pole Star is the only star that does not progress through the heavens (or in 2,500 BC, whatever cluster of stars in the north moves least), we would make the north-south line our first alignment, based on an alignment from the macehead at the center to the tripod a few feet away, due north.

> [The north-south line could also be determined by marking an alignment from the center to, again, twenty feet toward the sunrise point, and then a cord of the same length from the center to the sun's setting on the same day. Halve the distance between those two points, and a line from that center point back to the center of the circle would be the north-south line. Roughly. Solid knowledge of the triangle and its uses was necessary.]

So at the Ring itself the macehead of the backsight and the carved ball "mystery stone" of the foresight are dropped to a mark on the ground and pulled up to eye level. The sighting is done when the foresight (distant string) lines up with the backsight macehead and the putative Pole Star. A cord is stretched from the marks on the ground or the carved ball or stone, to fix the north-south line. The second orientation, which marks the equinoctial solar rising and setting (around September 21 and March 21) would easily be determined by the use of a 3-4-5 triangle and knotted cords. The triangle is placed with sides 3 or 4 on the north-south line. The 90 degree side points due east and west.

Sighting through backsight and foresight maceheads across to the Hills of Hoy

The Neolithic engineer, following the rising points of the sun from the central point of the circle, and marking particularly the equinox along with observation of the solstice points, could, within six months or so, with the use of triangles mark those alignments with cairns or standing stones or crevices in the hills beyond, and thus set up the basis for the primary alignment at the Ring: the summer solstice setting in the northwest that marked the entrance across the henge and into the center of the Ring. Use of triangles would have enabled the engineer to lay out the sightlines to the other three solstices, once the first had been observed, since the winter solstice set in the southwest is directly opposite the summer solstice rise in the northeast. Duplicating the angles in the southeast to arrive at the winter solstice rise also reveals the point in the northwest of the summer solstice sunset.

The north-south line is first set (see Figure 1); then the summer solstice sunrise in the northeast; then using the 3-4-5 triangle in the lower quadrant and, extending the blue lines to the same length, the winter solstice sunrise in the southeast is determined. Extending that orientation to the northwest yields the summer solstice setting; extending the northeast orientation to the southwest (Fig. 2) yields the winter solstice setting. Using the 3-4-5 triangle (Fig. 2) yields the equinox sunrise and sunset, due east and west. The triangle in Fig. 2 is shown in the same position as the triangle on the Large Orkney Stone.

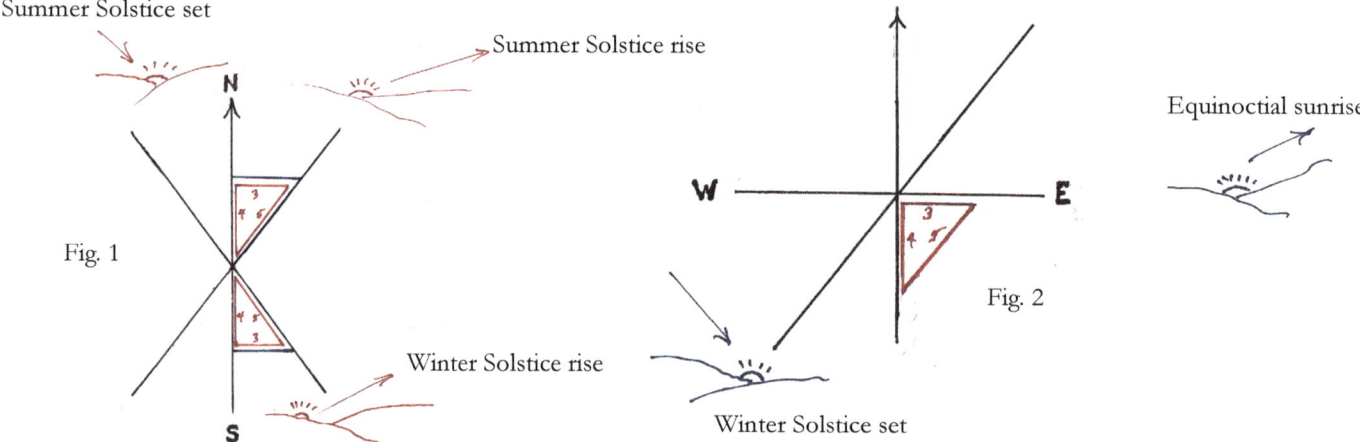

And it wasn't just the sun that was being observed at the Ring. When the vagaries of the moon are taken into account, as Alexander Thom has done definitively at many sites, we find a set of even more complex alignments related to the major and minor lunar standstills. In a paper presented to the Royal Institute of British Architects by Thom in 1977, he succinctly and vigorously defended his work on the solar and lunar sightlines at Brodgar: "The best site [to produce real proof that megalithic man used lunar observatories] is that at Brodgar in Orkney... The importance of the lunar observatories to megalithic man almost certainly lay in the fact that the observations he could make there assisted him in predicting eclipses."

At the Ring of Brodgar, looking toward the Hills of Hoy in the southwest

Putting aside those complexities of the lunar alignments as a given, and comparing the layout of the Large Stone with the layout of the Ring of Brodgar, we find several points of similarity.

The primary alignment of the Ring of Brodgar runs from the center of the Ring to the horizon point of the summer solstice setting in the northwest, crossing over the henge by means of a causeway. (The henge itself, some ten meters wide and 3.4 meters deep, is cut into solid rock in a grand perfect circle with a diameter of 103.7 meters.) The first notable feature of that alignment is that the orientation of the causeway is azimuth 335°. Likewise, the NW-SE incision on the Large Stone is at 335°. A second notable feature is the alignment of the small cairn near the southwestern part of the ditch, with the center of the Ring, and Fresh Knowe, which itself lies at the same distance from the edge of the Ring as the inside edge of the Ring is to the center. This alignment is close to the summer solstice rise, and the winter solstice set, and is therefore the mirror image of the primary alignment, the summer solstice set. And a third feature is that several parallel lines on the stone are matched by parallel alignments out at the Ring. Work in the field over a period of weeks would be required to ascertain the accuracy of these assertions, but the correspondences between the Large Orkney Stone and the Ring of Brodgar are clear. As we suggested earlier, the Stone was very likely used as a template for the Ring.

And down to Stonehenge

At this point we had discovered one feasible way to lay out a large stone circle, using the template of the Large Orkney Stone. If we move down to southern Britain and compare the template to the layout of Stonehenge, we will find several features in common, one of the most important of which is the use of parallel sightlines. The Station Stones of Stonehenge, which form a long rectangle, are the clearest example of the use of parallel sightlines: the pair of sightlines between 94 and 91, and between 93 and 92, point to the Southeast Major Moonrise and in the other direction to the Northwest Major Moonset, in the well-known 18.6 year cycle. The other pair, Station Stones 92 and 91, run parallel to the orientation of Station Stones 93 and 94, which align the Summer Solstice Rise and the Winter Solstice Set, and thus also run parallel to the primary axis of the monument: the solstice alignment that runs from the middle of the five trilithons, the center of the monument, to the Heel Stone. Comparison of the alignments of other complex sites will perhaps yield the same sort of pattern, a north-south line, orientations of solstices and major/minor moon events, where cairns and standing stones are planted at the site to enable parallel sightlines to be made and remembered. As we have seen, the large kerbstone at Loughcrew Cairn T near the Hag's Chair (p. 41) shows several parallel lines branching off at a solstice angle from a primary vertical cut.

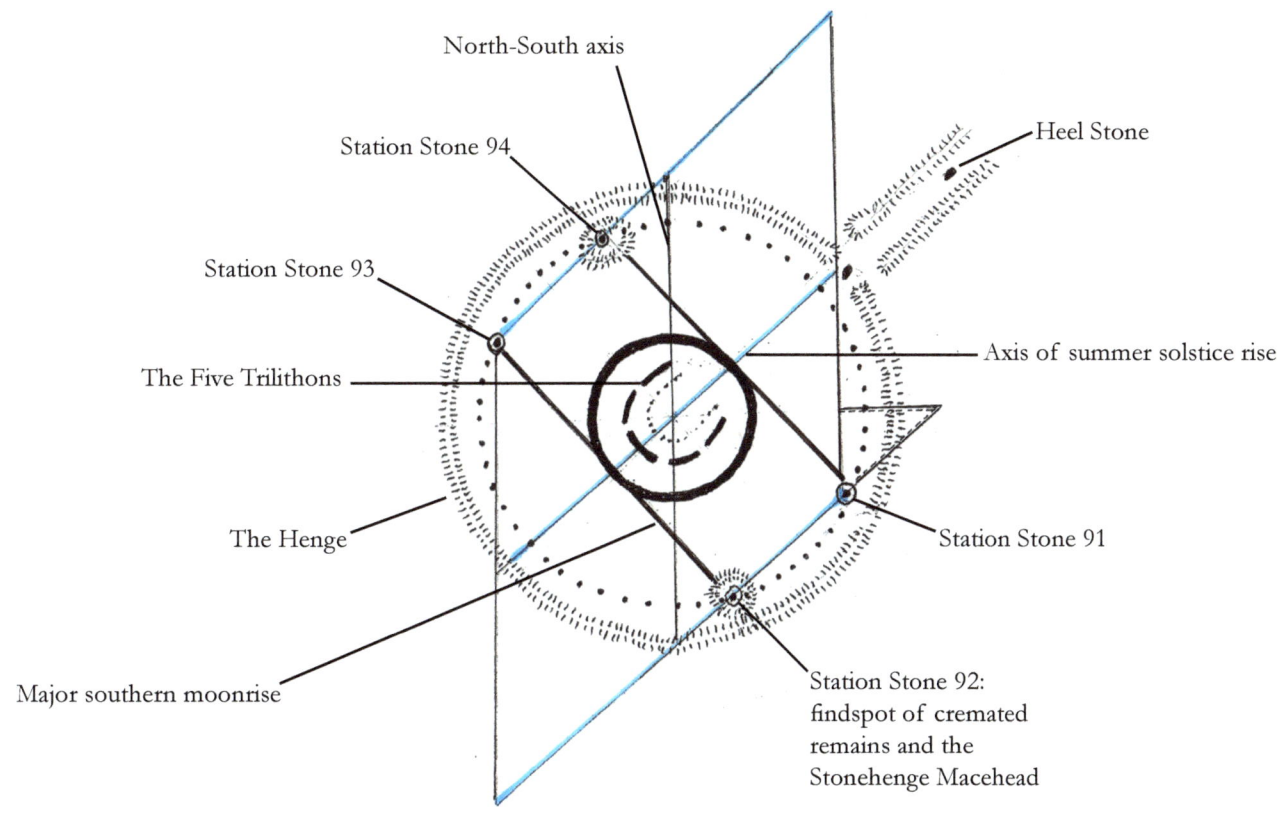

A diagram of Stonehenge and its major sightlines with the Large Orkney Stone lozenge superimposed

In addition to parallelisms, the importance of counting, measuring ratios, and orienting accurately is paramount in laying out a Stonehenge or a Brodgar: perhaps the six incisions across the upper third of Lozenge III on the Large Orkney Stone mark the relative distance between the center of the Ring of Brodgar and the edge of the Causeway, and between that point and the northeastern cairn known as Fresh Knowe, as we observed on the chart on page 48.

The alignment at Stonehenge between Station Stones 93 and 92, sighting to the Southwest, also runs over an important small cairn, just on the inside of the henge. A similar sightline at Brodgar from the center of the Ring passes over a cluster of some five small cairns that lie on the sightline of the NW-SE alignment, the winter solstice rise. (The distance of the cairns from the Southeast Causeway is twice the radius of the Ring. Again, understanding such ratios may have been the purpose of the six incisions on the Large Orkney Stone lozenge.) It would seem as if that alignment to the winter solstice rise was valuable real estate with everybody crowding in to get their little piece of the action. Other parallelisms and proportions may be revealed with more careful study, but let it suffice to say at that point that there seems to be a rather close correspondence between the layout of the various alignments at Stonehenge and the Ring of Brodgar, and the layout of the incisions on the Large Orkney Stone.

The Stonehenge Macehead at Station Stone 92

There is one more telling example of the conjunction of macehead, alignment, burial, orientation, and celestial event: In the outer ditch, in the henge of Stonehenge, at Station Stone 92, there was discovered a polished macehead, buried with cremated human remains. From Station Stone 93 in the northwest to Station Stone 92, that point on the ditch where the macehead was buried lines up with the sightline of the Major Southern Moonrise. Not a coincidence. What more appropriate way could there be of honoring an esteemed astronomer than to bury her cremated bones with the very tool, the beautiful macehead itself, that may have been the instrument of the discovery of that alignment: the once in 18.6 year moment in the cycle of the rising of the moon at its southernmost point. The Old People had a nice sense of propriety.

Stonehenge Macehead (with kind permission of Salisbury & South Wiltshire Museum ©)

OVER TO IRELAND AND NEWGRANGE

We have made a few speculations concerning the lines on the Stone, the Ring, and Stonehenge. But interlocking lozenges similar to those on the Large Orkney Stone are also to be found on *the* premier stone in the Neolithic carving tradition: Kerbstone 52 at Newgrange. Several features of K52 are noted: the lowest zigzag, the lattice of intersecting squares (not quite lozenges this time) on the lower left side of the stone, and on the right half rather a jumble of spirals, cups, rings, and tiny triangles scattered here and there. The deeply cut two inch wide vertical line from the bottom of the stone to the top divides K52 and matches the same line on Kerbstone 1, the entrance stone. This cut lines up with the axis of the tomb as a whole, which is oriented to the midwinter solstice, around December 21.

Model of Newgrange as it might have looked at the end of the 4th millenium BC (World Heritage Center, Newgrange)

The entrance of Newgrange, the largest tomb in Ireland, with the spiral-decorated Kerbstone 1 in the foreground and the roofbox above the entrance.

Closeup of the roofbox with lattice-decorated lintel. This opening permits the light to enter the center of the tomb around the time of the winter solstice.

Kerbstone 52, located on the Northwest point of the monument, directly opposite the Northeast entrance. The cut at the center of the stone, which is about 2 1/2 inches broad and reaches from top to bottom, matches the cut in the middle of Kerbstone 1. The lower left quadrant depicts four peaks of a zigzag, just below the lozenges and the three interfluent spirals above that. On the right side is a riot of spirals, cups, and moon-shaped carvings. A tripod set up a few feet beyond, and lining up with the center cut here and the center cut of Kerbstone 1 would orient the observer to the precise point on the Northwest horizon where the sun would set at the midsummer solstice. Kerbstone 52 is an abridged dictionary of Neolithic motifs.

Newgrange: Kerbstone 52

    An analysis of K52 would take us far beyond the scope of this discussion. Elizabeth Twohig, having analyzed the typologies of motifs, and speaking of megalithic art in general, states that "much of the art consists of geometric motifs which cannot be interpreted." But then goes on to say that "in general the geometric motifs seem likely to have had a specific meaning for those who carved them and possibly for those who saw them; these motifs should therefore be regarded as symbols . . . Megalithic art thus seems likely to have acted as a magico-religious symbolism, guarding the tombs and their contents and acting as a bond between those responsible for the monuments" (140). Andrew Jones in his study *Memory and Material Culture* concludes that "we need to consider the passage tomb art of the Boyne Valley monuments as a form of technology executed to instantiate the relationship between place and identity. On both the exterior and interior art acts as a 'technology of remembrance' because it is executed to memorialize the significance of place and identity. . . as forms of living archives" (188).

    Other scholars have made similar leaps into interpretation. For example, if one focuses on the left side of K52 just above the grass, one may speculate that the lowest zigzag represents the cycle of the rising and setting of the sun. Burl, MacKie, Twohig, Brennan, to name but a few, have also suggested such a meaning. And since the vertical line cut through the center of the Stone, as we have just noted, makes an alignment with a similar vertical line on Kerbstone 1 at the other side of the mound, aligning with the winter solstice sunrise in the southeast and the roofbox, then the lines of the lattice would be the north-south lines, and standing at near 90° angles, the equinox lines. Further, this K52 lattice can be seen to make a group of large interlocking lozenges, each made up of four smaller ones.

    Taken as a whole, Kerbstone 52 would appear to embody most of the essential motifs of the entire Neolithic tradition of stone carving: zigzags, cup marks, cup and rings, triangles, spirals, lunulas, the horseshoes (cf. the five great trilithons in the middle of Stonehenge), and the interlocking lozenges. Another template of orientations. If the Orkney Large Stone's intersecting lozenges were used to show the orientations of significant solstices and lunar standstills, the same was likely to be the case with the lattice of K52. The lozenges show the angles of alignment between the important orientations of the sun and the moon. All of these features are employed in both the astronomy and geometry of the builders.

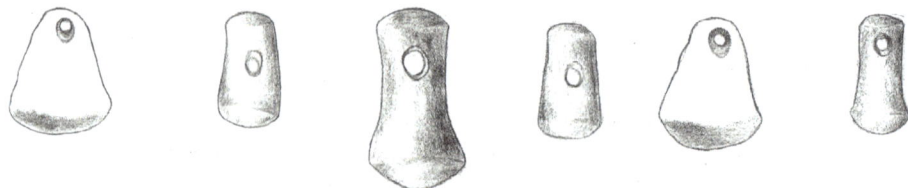

Drawings of amulets (ranging in size from 1-1.5" tall) found in the Newgrange chamber. They are miniatures of the macehead, further evidence that the maceheads were hung from a cord. (Hana Kurniawati)

Cup and rings, triangles, and various orientations of the carvings of K52

K52 lattice, with zigzag design at the bottom of the stone

Lattices and Spirals and Shamanism

Another interpretation of "rock art"—not astronomical—has been recently offered by Jeremy Dronfield, who has convincingly shown that the Neolithic lattice as well as other carvings functioned as a kind of "membrane" through which the shaman passed on the way to the Otherworld. Dronfield has also demonstrated that the spirals and zigzags found in so much Irish megalithic carving (most especially on K52 and the Knowth Macehead) have analogies to the shamanistic descent into the underworld. The famous Knowth Macehead, with its spirals for eyes, its hole for a mouth, its larger spirals for ears, and its lattice for hair and beard, is clearly anthropomorphic. When our theory of the astronomical use is combined with the concept of spirals as shamanistic motifs, we can envision the macehead as representing the shaman, headfirst on his journey, through trance, into the underworld, and we have the perfect conjunction of these theories in one artifact. The tops of Roe's Maesmore maceheads found in southern Britain may likewise depict hair, and therefore the same headfirst dive into the cave of the otherworld as the Knowth Macehead.

[In discussing Jeremy Dronfield's researches into polyoptic entopic imagery (the images reported to have been seen by the mind of the shaman, some of which geometrical images are not unlike the zigzag crescents seen during some migraine headaches), Lewis-Williams and Pearce state that this experience may indeed be the source of the imagery of the Neolithic passage tomb art—lattice, zigzag arcs, spirals— that "the carvings may thus have been a cryptographic 'text,' the correct exegesis of which was controlled by the elite and taught to selected novices, whose growing command of trance experience provided hallucinatory and deeply emotional guarantees of the truths they were learning" (277). One of the most remarkable zigzags is found on the Fourknocks I lintel stone, where the surface was carefully polished, as smooth and flat as a kitchen island marble table top, and then the zigzags pecked in with dramatic flair. The stone fairly leaps out at the observer.]

Knowth Macehead (published by permission ©National Museum of Ireland)

Closeup of the Fourknocks I Tomb Zigzag Stone

The Zigzag Stone inside the Fourknocks I Tomb

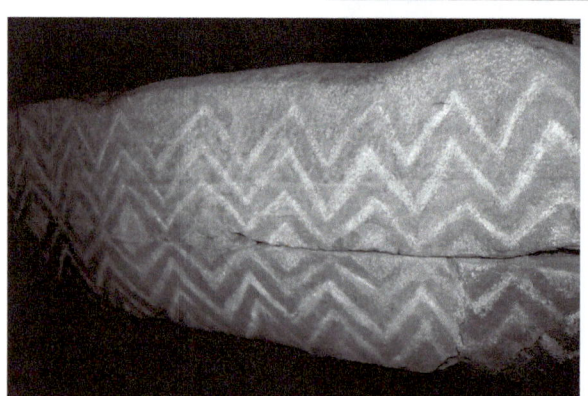

Lintel stones over the alcoves at Fourknocks I Tomb

Spiral carving in Loughcrew cairn T

It is not unreasonable to assert that there were practicing shamans in our period. They are found in some form in every early culture, as Miranda and Stephen Aldhouse-Green have shown. The chalk Folkton Drums, from the south of Britain, with their cups and rings, spirals, triangles, and intersecting lozenges are a product of this culture, and, like the maceheads and carved balls, would have been part of the priceless tools of the astronomer-shaman-elder.

The Drums are still described as a "mystery." There are lattices across the sides and beautiful spirals adorning the tops of the Drums. And there are several other examples of these designs from Neolithic Orkney, as well as from further south in Britain.

One of the three Folkton Drums, showing the anthropomorphic "eyes," large angles at the crossing, as well as lozenge latticework in the lower portion similar to that on the Large Orkney Stone (British Museum)

The drums could, of course, be functioning in several ways simultaneously: as a template for the layout of stone circles and other ritual spaces, as an icon of the relative angles of important celestial events on the horizon, as a membrane through which the elder in his/her function as shaman passed from our time and space through to the timelessness and spacelessness of the Otherworld of the Ancestors—for the purpose of consultation about the serious issues of the community and the future—when to move to the upper pastures, when to butcher the pig, whether the clan leader's niece should be taken by a neighbor's boy to live with his clan, when to transport the next desiccated or excarnated body into the tomb, and when to move the bones around again within the tomb. (Dronfield does not discuss cup and ring marks, since they are outside his topic, which is shamanism and its manifestation in Neolithic stone carving.) The ubiquity of spiral carvings and lattices in Ireland and Britain would suggest that shamanism was practiced throughout the lands. Towhig's authoritative statement, posted on the wall of the Visitor's Center at Newgrange, states the idea succinctly: "In general there is a very strong case for the argument in favour of some at least of the motifs in megalithic art being derived from altered states of consciousness." And the frequent proximity of spirals and lattices with cup and ring carvings would suggest that shamanism and astronomy were intertwined.

Who was in charge?

These concatenations of designs seemed to us further evidence of there being, as many archeologists have for some time been demonstrating, a North Atlantic culture of astronomers and engineers, not to mention those persons of power who controlled the planning and the gathering of resources, and supervised the construction and the usage of these places for the living and the dead. Atkinson suggested that the four Station Stones "form permanent and symbolic memorials of an operation of field-geometry which if it were repeated today, would tax the skill of many a professional surveyor." So everyone was working together on many different jobs on at least several levels. The cutting of the ditch at the Ring of Brodgar involved enormous effort but gave the people their ritual space. The orientations of the monuments required systematic observations and careful recording. The moving of stones demanded heroic physical effort. And the finer details of the buildings, for example, the corbelling of walls and ceilings, the slight upward rise of the Newgrange passage floor and the particular location of the roofbox, could hardly have been accomplished without the use of tools such as the macehead, plumb bob, and cup mark. On this issue of planning major monuments from start to finish, Renfrew and Bahn have stated that *"so far no archaeologist has sat down to work out in detail the minimum number of procedural steps that must have been planned in advance in undertaking major building works."* Perhaps the use of the macehead at Newgrange, both as orienting the tomb horizontally, and planning the entrance and the roof box vertically, would have made possible the high degree of accuracy evident in the monument. Perhaps in working out in detail such steps, an archeologist might begin with considering the potential uses of the tripod, macehead, and benchmark. After all, the sun shines through the roofbox down the passage and strikes just at the triple spiral on Orthostat 10 near the floor of the central chamber. Accurate planning in advance and certain "procedural steps" must have been accomplished to result in a Newgrange. We believe the macehead was an essential link in that process.

NEWGRANGE
This model of the construction of Newgrange shows the passage and central chambers with side alcoves. The sun shines through the roofbox, down the passage, gradually illuminating the carvings on the walls, and finally striking the spiral carving near the base of Orthostat 10 at the rear of the chamber during the days around December 21, the winter solstice. (World Heritage Center, Newgrange)

LOUGHCREW
The ruined cairn at Lough Crew is seen here from the top of Cairn T with a view towards the Wicklow Mountains beyond Dublin. This much smaller cairn, now open to the air, contains dozens of carvings of rock art in the remains of the central chamber. (photo: Kevin Champney)

RING OF BRODGAR
The Ring of Brodgar curves around with Salt Knowe at the right and the hills of Hoy in the distant background to the southwest. The main causeway points toward the setting sun at the summer solstice, as seen from the center of the Ring. Many of the stones still standing have been oriented toward various celestial events. The henge was cut through solid flagstone, and the whole monument is situated at one of the most evocative spots in the British Isles, with water all around and mountains in the distance.

CUWEEN HILL TOMB

Cuween Hill Tomb shows a superb example of a corbelled roof and capstone. The Neolithic builders of the Orkneys were most fortunate in the islands' abundance of red flagstone, which is mined in sheets throughout the Islands and then broken into the squared-off blocks that were used in the building of all the tombs. Measuring rods and maceheads—plumb bobs—would have been essential in determining the symmetry of the walls and corbelled roof. Who were the planners? How did the Orcadians gain their expertise in drystone masonary? Who made the decision to build in that particular variation of the chambered tomb and to orient it to the equinox sunrise directly opposite Wideford Hill Tomb several kilometers in the distance? And why bury twenty-four dogs' heads along with human remains?

TOWIE STONE

One can only stand in awe of the patience and skill of the macehead and stone ball grinders. Revealing skills comparable to a 19th century London-trained master engraver, several of our carved stones (e.g. Towie, Knowth) would be considered masterpieces in any age. We have little evidence of just how the engravers managed such feats. If quartz points were used in engraving, how were they held? Were they secured to a tool? Indeed, scatters and deposits of quartz have been found at several locations, not the least important of which are those at Skara Brae and Housesteads. The Towie Stone's carvings of spirals (as at Newgrange Kerbstone 1) and cup and ring incisions surpass all, and as we pointed out may have been part of the paraphernalia of the shaman as well as the astronomer. A high degree of style—proportion and attention to detail—is shown in much of the surviving stone tools and ceramics. (NMS)

STONEHENGE

At Stonehenge, apart from showing immense skills in astronomy and geometry, choices had to be made as to the area from whence they were to be hauled, which ones should be chosen for use, and how they were to be moved. Who supplied the hemp ropes required to lash a forty-ton stone to a sledge, to be dragged over twenty-six rolling miles (likely from the Marlborough area) across rough terrain to the site on the plain that had already been in ritual/astronomical use for over a thousand years. The inside surfaces are smooth, rubbed out stone against stone: an act of devotion, of penance, of compulsion? Who came up with the brilliant notion of applying the woodworker's mortise and tenon to stone? Since sandstone is one of the hardest of stones, how much time and perseverance did it take to pound out these devices and to make them fit? Contrary to received opinion (that the uprights were set up first), we suggest that perhaps the lintels were first raised on cribbing by levers and then the uprights set underneath, the lintels then being dropped down to fit the tenons. Sliding such a weight at such a height horizontally hardly seems feasible.

MEGAORIENTATIONS

The exacting skills of observation of our Neolithics are clearly seen in the mammoth size of the parts of the site plan and especially in the alignment of the Heel Stone and the opening at the foot of the middle trilithon. The sunlight-receptive "vessel," symbolized by the shape of the five trilithons—framing the alignment out to the northeast, the rising summer solstice, and the fading of the light six months later, at the setting of the winter solstice—shows the capability of early people to think "big," spatially, and to make the precise connections between earth and sky needed to order their lives.

ROCK ART

Many of the stones in the Boyne Valley, in the Newgrange area, evince what can only be described as art. A number of pre-historians have interpreted the motifs as symbols—rarely are the stone incisions and peckings "naturalistic." As in the case of the Paleolithic cave paintings, many Neolithic stone carvings are a palimpsest—one image over another. Other stones have been carefully laid out with a multitude of motifs, each occupying its own space. Someone or a powerful elite made thousands of decisions: How to orient the passage? Which stones are to be decorated? What are the motifs to be used?

SKARA BRAE
Skara Brae is a time capsule. Suddenly abandoned, the village kept intact much of its furniture, its tools, its jewelry, and the designs of its houses and passageways. Surely not everyone in Orkney could afford such luxuries. Was it a special settlement for an elite class of shamans and astronomers? The earliest excavators of the site thought so.

BEDSTEADS
Lozenges and lines of orientation are found incised on many tombs in Orkney and the Boyne Valley. The carvings on the bedsteads at Skara Brae are not mere random scratchings. Several surfaces show palimpsests, but each layer has its own motifs: triangles over lozenges over lines of orientation. While not graphemes, such practice was certainly a form of record keeping, according to our theory.

AVEBURY

Avebury is the largest henge in the Isles. The ditch is more than a mile in circumference. The ditch is 25 feet deep, cut as a V through the chalk, but with a floor some six feet wide, flat and polished. Causeways show that the ditch was not first intended for defensive purposes. The standing stones weigh over 30 tons each. Along with West Kennet Barrow nearby, the largest barrow in Britain, and Silbury Hill, the largest man-made structure in Europe from any age, the Avebury area stands out as one of the most important ceremonial centers in the British Isles. It is contemporaneous with Newgrange, the earliest phases of Stonehenge, and the large Orkney monuments, such as the Ring of Brodgar and Maeshowe. Who was dreaming up these gargantuan projects? Who was organizing the sarsen-hauling operation? Who knew enough physics and geometry to raise the stones and drop them into their sockets, carved as the reverse of the lower third of the stones? Was he a Michelangelo of "negative sculpture"? One can only stand in awe of the determination of a people that lasted through several generations before completion of the monument. Were they some of the same forty-six people whose bones were disinterred at West Kennet Barrow only a couple of miles away? (© English Heritage Photo Library)

SILBURY HILL
This mammoth mound is the largest man-made structure in Europe. Twelve stories in height, Silbury Hill was built with chalk blocks cut from the area around the base of the monument. Excavations through the base to the center and from the top of the mound to original soil at the base have revealed no trace of burial. Various bits of organic matter— plant material and Mayflies— found throughout the mound give clues as to the dates of its construction (3200 BC onward), the time of year it was under construction, and approximately how many years it was in progress. In mythology and early history the mound was reputed to be the burial place of King Sil. Some writers have suggested that the mound, as viewed from above, represents the pregnant womb of Mother Earth, with the excavated area, a wetland, representing her body. (photo: Siri Jones).

MODEL OF SILBURY HILL
Building up a series of concentric walls with spokes radiating from the center as shown in the model and with chalk rubble as in-fill, the monument has stood intact for four thousand years. The summit would have been a superb backsight point, with long views toward the foresights in every direction. Something powerful must have compelled these people to undertake such a long-term project. Who came up with its unique structure? How many laborers were involved? Who was the general contractor?

Ring of Brodgar (photo: Ana Ottoson)

All Together now: The Neolithic Powertool Kit

In summary, what we observed in our journey were several pieces of a puzzle, each piece of which was more or less inexplicable in and of itself, but which seemed to fit remarkably well together with all the rest of the pieces. The frequent museum designation "mystery stone" or "ritual object" shows that we don't really know what these things are all about. These artifacts have not been wanting in theorists like ourselves who try to explain their use. But when the pieces are placed in the context of other types of carvings, of the orientations, the circles, the houses, the spirals, zigzags, lattices, tripods, and maceheads—they seem to fit together, and, taken as a whole, manifest what surely would have been an integral part of their ritual, spiritual, and common life.

If the components are working together, the macehead fits the cup; the sight hole in the macehead frames the view in the distance and could be turned and narrowed to protect the eye against the rays of the sun; the tripod enables an absolute vertical from which can be determined the horizontal alignments; the stone stakes mark the points and hold the cords; the carved balls serve as weights as well as benchmarks, and the macehead in conjunction with the ball hanging from the second tripod could have been adjusted to observe the height of the sun or moon in the sky at any point during the day or night. Or for adjusting the height of the roofbox at Newgrange. Or the height and length of the passageway at Maeshowe. With two tripods, cup and ring, and macehead, a point in the distance can be easily fixed. The lightness of the tripod (of sticks or pvc) enables its quick and easy movement, so as to make fine adjustments and more accurate orientations.

Back at Skara Brae the alignments are carved into the Large Orkney Stone, and over at Newgrange many designs, including latticework, are carved into K52. Both show the perfect conjunction of the astronomical and the shamanistic. From a technical point of view, it would have been the cup and ring, tripod, and macehead that enabled such levels of accuracy to be achieved: At Stonehenge, the observer at the center sees the last glimmer of light in the crevice at the narrow setting of the uprights of the middle and largest trilithon, where the bottom corner of the right orthostat and the level ground just catch, accurately, the last rays of the winter solstice setting sun. Or at Newgrange, where the gradual raising of the floor enables the midwinter solstice rising sun to strike near the bottom of orthostat C10 in the central chamber, where the famous triple spiral is pecked out on the stone just above the floor. In these two examples alone we see several remarkable feats of alignment as well as the undoubted need of our people to make a connection with the heavenly bodies. It was this connection that enabled the people to set their daily lives in harmony with the terrestrial and celestial order, a lesson that we 21st century greedmongers and wasters could learn from in this age of impending ecological disaster. The uses of these tools in the planting of crops, the orientation of houses, the placement of the excarnated bones or, later, cremations, into houses for the dead, along with the ritual life of the people—all pieces of a puzzle, which seem to fit into a whole and show us at least a glimpse into the working of the mind of the Neolithic farmer.

As we look back over some of the dogmas that have informed Neolithic study for many years, they become, when seen against the speculations offered here, quite untenable: The macehead was mounted on a pole, carried with swagger over the clan chieftan's shoulder as he strutted about the stones? The macehead was jammed on a stick like a little stone battle axe to smash the skulls of the enemy? The bedstead carvings at Skara Brae are mere random scratchings? The cup and rings were pounded out by farmers with way too much time on their hands? Our Stone Age ancestors were indifferent to the precise motions of the "greater and lesser lights" and in any case were incapable of exacting observations to within one degree of azimuth (as the roofbox at Newgrange) or one centimeter of distance in the layouts of their monuments (as in the mortise and tenons at Stonehenge)?

No. If our theory is correct, the maceheads and carved balls were valuable and beautiful tools, essential to the Neolithic astronomer, architect, and shaman. The carvings of Skara Brae and Knowth are much too precise and time-intensive to be mere scratchings or art for art's sake. The monuments themselves, from little Unstan Tomb or great Maeshowe, to Stonehenge or Newgrange, are so precisely laid out and oriented as to baffle even the most astute observers. And it all happened with plumb bobs, tripods, cords, stakes, benchmarks, and "blueprints" incised in stone.

The theory is simple and practical and elegant, and can account for virtually every aspect of Neolithic esoterica. The Early People gallery (National Museums Scotland) does have most of the pieces of the puzzle exhibited, but the identification boards always fall back on the terms "mystery stone" or "ritual object." Are we imposing an order and meaning on these "mystery stones"? Perhaps. Hamlet's conversation with Polonius reminds us that the "meaning" of art ultimately lies in the eye of the beholder, our speculating eye, viewpoint, our "mind's eye." But it may also be that the single cord, pulled down by a macehead to the stone cup on an outcrop offers the best starting point for the next level of our understanding of these amazing people of the Isles. As for our next Scotland Tour, we will be measuring the radial cuts on the next group of cup and rings at Achnabreck Farm near Kilmartin. And hoping for warmer weather.

The author standing in front of West Kennet Barrow, near Avebury, in 1990 (photo: Siri Jones)

Scotland Tour IV at the Ring of Brodgar, with two sets of tripods, two maceheads, and a 3-4-5 triangle, April, 2007

Scotland Tour II, Edinburgh, February 2005

Ireland Tour, Loughcrew Cairn, April 2008

References

Aldhouse-Green, Miranda and Stephen. *The Quest for the Shaman: Shape-shifters, Sorcerers and Spirit-healers of Ancient Europe.* London: Thames and Hudson, 2005.

Argyll: Islay, Jura, Colonsay & Oronsay. Edinburgh: The Royal Commission on the Ancient and Historical Monuments of Scotland, 1984.

Barclay, Alistair. "Grooved Ware from the Upper Thames Region," in *Grooved Ware in Britain and Ireland,* eds. Rosamund Cleland and Ann MacSween. Oxford and Oakville, Ct.: Oxbow Books, 1999.

Beckensall, Stan. *Prehistoric Rock Art in Northumberland.* Charleston, SC: Tempus Publishing Inc., 2001.

Bradley, Richard, Tim Phillips, Colin Richards, and Matilda Webb. "Decorating the Houses of the Dead: Incised and Pecked Motifs in Orkney Chambered Tombs." *Cambridge Archaeological Journal* 11:1 (2000), 45-67.

Bradley, Richard. *The Good Stones: a new investigation of the Clava Cairns.* Edinburgh: Society of Antiquaries of Scotland, 2000.

Bradley, Richard with Chris Ball, Sharon Croft, and Tim Phillips. "The stone circles of northeast Scotland in the light of excavation." *Antiquity* 76 (2003), 840.

Bradley, Richard and Robert Chapman. "The nature and development of long-distance relations in Later Neolithic Britain and Ireland," in *Peer Polity Interaction and Socio-political Change,* eds. Colin Renfrew and John F. Cherry. Cambridge: Cambridge University Press, 1986.

Bradley, Richard. *Rock Art and the Prehistory of Atlantic Europe.* London: Routledge, 1997.

Bradley, Richard. *The Past in Prehistoric Societies.* London: Routledge, 2002.

Brennan, Martin. *The Boyne Valley Vision.* Mountrath, Portlaoise, Ireland: The Dolmen Press, 1980.

Burl, Aubrey. *Prehistoric Astronomy and Ritual.* Princes Risborough, Buckinghamshire: Shire Publications, 1997.

Burl, Aubrey. *Prehistoric Avebury.* New Haven and London: Yale University Press, 1979.

Childe, V. Gordon. *Ancient dwellings at Skara Brae.* Edinburgh: Her Majesty's Stationery Office, l950.

Childe, V. Gordon. *Skara Brae, A Pictish Village in Orkney.* London: Kegan Paul, Trench, Trubner & Co., Ltd., 1931.

Clarke, Ann. "The Stone Tool Assemblage," in *Dwelling among the Monuments,* ed. Colin Richards.

Clarke, D. V. *The Neolithic Village at Skara Brae, Orkney, 1972-73 Excavations: an interim report.* Edinburgh: Her Majesty's Stationery Office, 1976.

Clarke, D. V., T. G. Cowie and A. Foxon. *Symbols Of Power At The Time Of Stonehenge.* Edinburgh: National Museum of Antiquities of Scotland, 1985.

Cooney, Gabriel. *Looking at the Irish Neolithic.* London and New York: Routledge, 2000.

Cummings, Vicki and Alasdair Whittle. "Tombs with a view: landscape, monuments and trees." *Antiquity* 77 (2003), 255.

David, Nicholas, Judy Sterner, and Kodzo Gavua."Why Pots are Decorated." *Current Anthropology* 29 (June 1988), 365.

Davies, Norman. *The Isles.* Oxford: Oxford University Press, 1999.

Downes, Jane and Colin Richards. "The Dwellings at Barnhouse," in *Dwelling among the Monuments,* ed. Colin Richards.

Downes, Jane, Sally M. Foster, and C. R. Wicknam-Jones. *Heart of Neolithic Orkney World Heritage Site: Research agenda.* Edinburgh: Historic Scotland, 2005.

Dronfield, Jeremy. "Subjective vision and the source of Irish megalithic art." *Antiquity* 69 (1995), 539.

Dronfield, Jeremy. "Entering Alternative Realities: Cognition, Art and Architecture in Irish Passage-Tombs." *Cambridge Archaeological Journal* 6:1 (1996), 37-72.

Edmonds, Mark. "Their Use is Wholly Unknown," in *Vessels for the Ancestors*, eds. Niall Sharpton and Alison Sheridan.

Eogan, George. *Knowth and the passage-tombs of Ireland*. London: Thames and Hudson Ltd., 1986.

Eogan, George, "Knowth before Knowth." *Antiquity* 72 (1998), 162.

Foxen, Andrew. *Neolithic and Bronze Age Finds*. Unpublished. Orkney Library.

Garnham, Trevor. *Lines on the Landscape—Circles from the Sky: Monuments of Neolithic Orkney*. Strould, Gloucestershire: Tempus Publishing, 2004.

Hayman, Richard. *Riddles in Stone: Myths, Archaeology and the Ancient Britons*. London and Rio Grande: The Hambledon Press, 1997.

Hedges, John W. *Tomb of the Eagles: A Window on Stone Age Tribal Britain*. London: John and Erika Hedges, 2000.

Helms, Mary. "Tangible Materiality and Cosmological Other in the Development of Sedentism," in *Rethinking materiality: the engagement of mind with the material world*, eds. Elizabeth DeMarrais, Chris Gosden, and Colin Renfrew. Cambridge: The McDonald Institute for Archeological Research, 2004.

Henshall, A. S. and J. N. G. Ritchie. *The Chambered Cairns of the Central Highlands: An Inventory of the Structures and their Contents*. Edinburgh: Edinburgh University Press, 2001.

Hodder, Ian and Scott Hutson. *Reading the Past: Current Approaches to Interpretation in Archaeology*. Cambridge: Cambridge University Press, 2003.

Jones, Andrew. *Memory and Material Culture*. Cambridge: Cambridge University Press, 2007.

Lawson, Andrew J. "Stonehenge: creating a definitive account." *Antiquity* 66 (1992), 934.

Lewis-Williams, David and David Pearce. *Inside the Neolithic Mind*. London: Thames and Hudson, 2005.

MacKie, Euan. *The Megalithic Builders*. Oxford: Phaedon Press, 1977.

MacKie, Euan W. Response: "The structure and skills of British Neolithic Society: a brief response to Clive Ruggles & Gordon Barclay." *Antiquity* 76 (2002), 666.

MacKie, Euan W. "Maeshowe and the winter solstice: ceremonial aspects of the Orkney Grooved Ware culture." *Antiquity* 71 (1997), 338.

Moffat, Alistair. *Before Scotland: The story of Scotland before history*. New York: Thames and Hudson, 2005.

Morris, Ronald W. B. *The Prehistoric Rock Art of Argyll*. Poole, Dorset: The Dolphin Press, 1977.

Morris, Ronald W. B. *The Prehistoric Rock Art of Galloway and the Isle of Man*. Poole, Dorset: Blandford Press, 1979.

Norris, Ray. "Megalithic observatories in Britain: real or imagined?" in *Records in Stone*, ed. C. L. N. Ruggles. Cambridge: Cambridge University Press, 1988, 2002.

O'Kelly, Michael J. *Newgrange: Archaeology, art and legend*. London: Thames and Hudson, 1984.

O'Sullivan, Muiris. *Metalithic Art in Ireland*. Dublin: Town House and Country House, 1993.

Parker Pearson, M. and Ramilisonina. "The stones pass on the message." *Antiquity* 72 (1998), 308.

Piggott, Stuart. *The Neolithic Cultures of the British Isles*. Cambridge: Cambridge University Press, 1954.

Piggott, Stuart. *Ancient Europe from the beginnings of Agriculture to Classical Antiquity*. Edinburgh: Edinburgh University Press, 1965.

Renfrew, Colin. *British Prehistory: A New Outline*. London: Gerald Duckworth and Co. Ltd., 1974.

Renfrew, Colin. "Varna and the emergence of wealth in prehistoric Europe," in *The social life of things: Commodities in cultural perspective*, ed. Arjun Appadurai. Cambridge: Cambridge University Press, 1986.

Renfrew, Colin. *Archaeology and Language: The Puzzle of Indo-European Origins*. London: Jonathan Cape, 1987.

Renfrew, Colin, ed. *The Prehistory of Orkney*. Edinburgh: Edinburgh University Press, 1993.

Renfrew, Colin and Paul Bahn. *Archaeology: Theories Methods and Practice*. New York and London: Thames and Hudson, 2000.

Renfrew, Colin and Paul Bahn. *Archaeology: The Key Concepts*. Abingdon, Oxon: Routledge, 2005.

Richards, Colin. "The Neolithic Settlement of Orkney," in *Dwelling among the Monuments*, ed. Colin Richards.

Richards, Colin, ed. *Dwelling among the Monuments: the Neolithic village of Barnhouse, Maeshowe passage grave and surrounding monuments at Stenness, Orkney*. Cambridge: McDonald Institute for Archaeological Research, 2005.

Ritchie, Anna and Graham Ritchie. *The ancient monuments of Orkney*. Edinburgh: Her Majesty's Stationery Office, 1995.

Ritchie, Graham, ed. *The Archaeology of Argyll*. Edinburgh: Edinburgh University Press, 1997.

Ritchie, Graham and Anna Ritchie. *Scotland: Archaeology and Early History*. Edinburgh: Edinburgh University Press, 1991.

Ritchie, Anna. *Prehistoric Orkney*. London: B. T. Batesford/Historic Scotland, 1995.

Ritchie, Roy. "Stone Axeheads and Cushion Maceheads fromn Orkney and Shetland: Some Similarities and Contrasts," in *Vessels for the Ancestors*, eds. Niall Sharpton and Alison Sheridan.

Roe, Fionna. "Stone mace-heads and the latest Neolithic cultures of the British Isles," in *Studies in Ancient Europe: Essays presented to Stuart Piggott*, eds. J. M. Coles and D. D. A. Simpson. Bristol: Leicester University Press, l968.

Rots, Veerle. "Towards an understanding of hafting: the macro- and microscopic evidence." *Antiquity* 77 (2003), 805.

Ruggles, Clive and Aubrey Burl. "A New Study of the Aberdeenshire Recumbent Stone Circles." *Archaeoastronomy* 8 (1985), 25-60.

Ruggles, C. L. N., ed. *Records in Stone: Papers in memory of Alexander Thom*. Cambridge: Cambridge University Press, 1988.

Ruggles, Clive. *Astronomy in Prehistoric Britain and Ireland*. New Haven and London: Yale University Press, 1999.

Scarre, Chris. "Sound, Place and Space: Towards an Archaeology of Acoustics," in *Archaeoacoustics*, eds. Chris Scarre and Graeme Lawson. Cambridge: McDonald Institute for Archaeological Research, 2006.

Sharpton, Niall and Alison Sheridan. *Vessels for the Ancestors*. Edinburgh: Edinburgh Univerity Press, 1992.

Simpson, Derek and Rachel Ransom. "Macheads and the Orcadian Neolithic," in *Vessels for the Ancestors*, eds. Niall Sharpton and Alison Sheridan.

Stevenson, J. B. "The Prehistoric Rock Carvings of Argyll," in *The Archaeology of Argyll*, ed. Graham Ritchie. Edinburgh: Edinburgh University Press, 1997.

Thom, Alexander. "Megalithic geometry in standing stones." *New Scientist,* 12 March, 1964.

Thom, Alexander. "Observatories in ancient Britain." *New Scientist,* 2 July, 1964.

Thom, Alexander. "Time-keeping with standing stones." *New Scientist,* 29 December, 1966.

Thom, Alexander. *Megalithic Sites in Britain*. Oxford: Oxford University Press, 1967.

Thom, Alexander. *Megalithic Lunar Observatories*. Oxford: Oxford University Press, 1971.

Thom, Alexander. "Megalithic Astronomy." Paper given 6 September 1977 to the Royal Institute of British Architects.

Twohig, Elizabeth Shee. *The Megalithic Art of Western Europe*. Oxford: Clarendon Press, 1981.

www.ingramcontent.com/pod-product-compliance
Lightning Source LLC
Chambersburg PA
CBHW041515220426
43668CB00002B/29